TOWARDS A GENEALOGY OF SPECTACLE

TOWARDS A GENEALOGY OF SPECTACLE

understanding contemporary spectacular experiences

YUNUS TUNCEL

with an introduction by
RAINER J. HANSHE

EYECORNER PRESS

© Yunus Tuncel & EyeCorner Press | 2011

Towards a Genealogy of Spectacle:
Understanding contemporary spectacular experiences

Introduction © Rainer J. Hanshe

Published by EYECORNER PRESS, March 2011

ISBN: 978-87-92633-07-1

Cover design and layout: Camelia Elias
Fragments of Greek Theater

Dedicated to

My parents

Meltem and Mayra

Cem Aydoğan

Avignon Theater Festival

Spectacle is the crystallization of the desire of human beings to view, or to experience, one another in a collective body and as in a festival.

CONTENTS

Preface | 9
Introduction by Rainer J. Hanshe | 11
Author's Introduction | 35

§§§

Part I: Unity of Spectacle: The Outer Forces of Spectacle | 41
Part II: Unity of Spectacle: The Inner Forces of Spectacle | 51

    Chapter 1: Ecstasy | 51
    Chapter 2: Illusion, Image, and Symbol | 59
    Chapter 3: Imagination | 69
    Chapter 4: Myth, Religion, and the Aura | 72
    Chapter 5: Feelings, Emotions, Violence, and Catharsis | 78
    Chapter 6: The Unconscious and Transference in the Body and the Soul | 86
    Chapter 7: Movement | 91
    Chapter 8: Language, Text, Music, and Image | 94
    Chapter 9: Science and Technology | 100
    Chapter 10: Thinking and the Intellect | 103
    Chapter 11: Space and Place | 106
    Chapter 12: Time and Temporality | 119
    Appendix to Parts I and II: The Unity of Spectacle and the Question of Spectacular Power | 113

Part III: Grand Artistic Spectacle and the Total Artwork | 121
Epilogue | 135

Appendix 1: Important characteristics of the Greek tragic spectacle at its height | 146

Appendix 2: THE UNITY OF SPECTACULAR EXPERIENCES: PROPOSAL FOR A PROGRAM OF ACTION
A MANIFESTO | 149

Notes | 156

Author's Preface

What is spectacle? This question, simple and complex at the same time, has intrigued me for more than ten years and led me to a path of research, new experiences of spectacles, and teaching as I posed new questions on the way. There can be no easy definition or a simple understanding of such a complex phenomenon of culture that is also *historically* determined. My main concern throughout this research has been to make an attempt at an understanding of the forces that are at work in spectacular experiences within the context of history of ideas and debates pertinent to the topic. To take even the smallest step, I had to narrow down my project to 1) the western context (with due respect to other spectacular forms from which we can learn so that we can critically reflect on our own), and 2) artistic spectacles (while I tried to avoid aesthetic theories to the extent that it is possible). Out of this condensed framework, I sometimes take the liberty to explore other issues that were not part of the earlier investigation.

In today's world, thousands of spectacles are being made and are experienced by millions of people; spectacle is everywhere. This is not to say that all of these spectacles are on any grand scale. Although spectacle is pervasive in contemporary society, it is also the least understood phenomenon of culture. We are all in it and shaped by it to a large extent, but we understand it only poorly. In my research I wanted to attack this question and bring out some of the essential problems that are ingrained into our pathos of spectacle today.

Although the works of many artists and philosophers reveal much about the question of spectacle, I find them limited or short-sighted, or, in many cases, this question was treated only marginally as it was subordinated to other philosophically more pressing questions. On the other hand, contemporary (that is, post-WW II) theoreticians such as Adorno, Horkheimer, Debord, Barthes, Baudrillard, or Foucault who deal with the subject more comprehensively, reflect on one type of spectacle or another, as they either evade the broader question or pretend that they have dealt with it. One can no doubt learn from their works (which I have), but in none of them have I found the question of spectacle explored in-depth, in a multi-faceted way. This gave me some frustration, but also an impetus to do my own thinking.

A theoretical work has its merits if it is soaked in concrete experiences. Like many of my contemporaries, I too have experienced many artistic spectacles some of which had a lasting impression on my soul. There was no room to give an account of all these experiences; however, upon suggestions by my friends, I decided to include some of these experiences in the footnotes where I thought they would be pertinent to what is being said in the theoretical part. Although sometimes these examples may be hazy, arbitrary, or too obvious, I decided to include them to make some of my theoretical speculations more concrete.

Finally, although the book is of a theoretical nature, I do not expect my readers to be only theoreticians, but also spectacle-makers and spectators who wish to think through one of the acute problems of our age, a problem undoubtedly connected to its larger questions.

THE NECESSITY OF ILLUSION

by
RAINER J. HANSHE

> *Go, go, go, said the bird: human kind*
> *Cannot bear very much reality.*
> *Time past and time future*
> *What might have been and what has been*
> *Point to one end, which is always present.*
> —T.S. Eliot, "Burnt Norton"

> *If the word had not lost its strict meaning, I would call the new art a spiritual art. A mental art, then, which will demand of the reader and the listener the sensitivity and the imagination of a performer who, like the musicians of India, is also a creator.*
> —Octavio Paz, "Invention, Underdevelopment, Modernity"

To Guy Debord, spectacle is "a specious form of the sacred."[1] As a material reconstruction of religious illusion, it remains metaphysical, with the image or illusion, as manifested in whatever form of spectacle, substituting God. In place of the genuflecting believer is the passive spectator, who takes the spectacle for the highest or purest form of reality. Illusion's power to supplant reality makes it extremely dangerous, a threat to existence itself, as was the most treacherous and nihilistic illusion, metaphysics, which falsified, devalued, and negated reality for nearly 2000 years. Despite the convenient optimism of many, the repercussions of metaphysics

---

1 Guy Debord, *The Society of the Spectacle* (NY: Zone Books, 1994), p. 20 or §25.

continue to persist, for if Nietzsche diagnosed the ascetic ideal at work even in atheism and science, can we be certain that we have completely freed ourselves of that powerful an illusion? In Debord's desire to not only harm spectacular society but to destroy it there is something of the Nietzschean hammering at idols, for he was in combat with one of the most pernicious shadows of the dead God. In the epoch of virtual reality, the hazard of reality being overtaken by illusion could not be more angst-ridden a menace. But then, ontologically, reality can never be overtaken; the threat is actually in permitting image and illusion to dominate and supersede the *perception* of reality. In our highly mediated society, to Debord, life itself is merely a spectacular reconstruction of reality, which is no longer or rarely lived directly—illusion has made reality supernatural and illusion natural. We are no longer in the world, but in our projection of it. The spectacle is ubiquitous.

To shift from the metaphysical to the aesthetic realm, though for Debord aesthetics remains largely metaphysical, if facsimiles or clones of Lascaux and Altamira are, *perhaps*, necessary critical interventions against the erasure or disappearance of our cultural heritage, what is to be made of the cloning of paintings not in immediate danger of decay? With Factum Arte's cloning of Caravaggio's works and Veronese's *Wedding at Cana*, we have two startling examples to ponder. As a culture, are we to resort to the cloning of artworks in an attempt to ameliorate acts of cultural appropriation, like Napoleon's, if actual reparation is even possible? Is not—or rather, *was* not the very absence of Veronese's painting in the Palladian Refectory of San Giorgio Maggiore, Venice, a necessary absence, a felt physical *marker*, not a *signifier*, of appropriation and loss? To Artaud, even if a work is lost or destroyed its force and energy remain: "The library at Alexandria can be burnt down. There are forces above and beyond papyrus: we may temporarily be deprived of our ability to discover these forces, but their energy will not be suppressed."[2] The same possibility of destruction exists for all art, especially painting, and although this dilemma is different, if a painting or any other artwork is too fragile to be returned to its country of origin, must that loss not be continually suffered? The public's willingness to pay to experience a clone in lieu of visiting an original—which is being done with Veronese's painting—is indicative of an aesthetic if not moral and ethical crisis. Even knowing it was a clone one Italian still exulted over it, proclaiming that "the Veronese" had at last returned home . . . And what if museums and galleries begin cloning artworks as a form of insurance, displaying clones instead of original artworks in order to protect what to them is not primarily an aesthetic object but a financial commodity?[3] Or in the desire for perfection, we begin 'correcting' artworks, as actually has been done, supposedly appending what has vanished, restoring 'original' coloration, and altering what time has erased?[4] Time will keep erasing the new surface; disaster cannot be staved off; decay is inexorable; life and death are indissolubly bound. If one day we become so expert at cloning, it may never be possible to discern with the naked eye the difference between a clone and an

---

2 Antonin Artaud, *The Theater and Its Double* (New York: Grove Press, 1958), 10.

3 Considering the fact that, after stumbling, a female tourist made a six inch tear with her umbrella in Picasso's "The Actor" (1905) while visiting the Metropolitan Museum of Art in early 2010, such unethical practices may not be so surprising. Although such accidents are rare, artworks have suffered both accidental and deliberate vandalism, the latter generally by inferior artists who are threatened by exceptional works of art.

4 Is this not a primarily Western anxiety? In opposition, consider the Japanese aesthetic of *wabi-sabi*, which "represents the exact opposite of the Western ideal of great beauty as something monumental, spectacular, and enduring. Wabi-sabi is not found in nature at moments of bloom and lushness, but at moments of inception or subsiding." See Leonard Koren, *Wabi-Sabi for Artists, Designers, Poets & Philosophers* (California: Stone Bridge Press, 1994), 50.

original. But isn't there something that always betrays the replicant? Isn't this a question of perspicacity, of the keenness of one's senses, the sharpness of one's intellect? If some spectators may be deceived, others will not, and this is a question of cultivation, which is one of the fundamental concerns threaded throughout Yunus Tuncel's investigation of spectacle.

Yet, for many, there is no disquiet, no dis-ease, no anxiety. In his lecture at the Park Avenue Armory in New York City on cloning masterpieces, Adam Lowe, the founder of Factum Arte, expressed no apprehension regarding his work, and to validate and affirm it he emphasized the immediate and stirring emotional reaction of the audience that first witnessed the unveiling of the Veronese clone in 2007.[5] He also claimed that the public response to it was "almost universally positive."[6] Quality however cannot be quantified numerically or validated by mass emotional responses, nor by an amorphous public whose degree of cultivation cannot be determined through such observations, nor, to say the least, with dubious electronic devices. During his lecture Lowe referred to Walter Benjamin's notion of the aura and claimed that when the original Veronese was measured with an "aura meter" it registered

---

5 When discussing the Veronese reproduction in 2007, Lowe rejected the term "clone" and argued that his work was instead "a deep and detailed study" whereas the title of the lecture he presented at the Armory on 1 December 2010, "Duplicating da Vinci: The Art of Cloning a Masterpiece," clearly indicates his new acceptance of it. How a facsimile is a study is rather questionable for studies are not seemingly exact replicas but have something personal in them, new thoughts, new ideas, new interpretations, questions. On the Veronese clone, see Elisabetta Povoledo, "A Painting Comes Home (or at Least a Facsimile)," *New York Times*, 29 September 2007. On Lowe's lecture at the Armory: http://www.armoryonpark.org/index.php/programs_events/detail/duplicating_da_vinci/

6 http://www.factum-arte.com/eng/conservacion/caravaggio/caravaggio_progress.asp

an aura of 75% whereas when the clone was measured it registered an aura of 100%. Precisely what was being measured was not clarified, but after recounting this anecdote, Lowe earnestly suggested discarding Benjamin's essay and declared it to be of little legitimacy. Aura however is not something metaphysical for Benjamin and isn't limited to or solely defined by some unquantifiable (or perhaps quantifiable) element but also relates specifically to the physical painting itself as a unique object, one whose history can be traced through time from owner to owner, so it involves a genetic history, including the damage the painting has suffered, how it has disintegrated or naturally decayed over time, its specific spatial placement, etc. If aesthetics and archeology here begin to merge—or clash, the point is that the biography of a work assists with establishing its historical veracity. The tangible aesthetic matter however devolves around the singular hand-crafted object as a physical manifestation of thought. How that is measured and what makes it evident is the crucible by which all of this rises or falls. One way by which to gauge this without resorting to seemingly mystifying principles such as Benjamin's notion of the aura is to analyze how the artist's thought is manifested in his or her work. If something is genuine, it has a certain geometric harmony, which is to say it is perfectly congruent with itself: all of its markings reveal the thought of a single mind. Although certain artists often had apprentices completing parts of their work, the conception and overall design of the work betrays a distinct and personal vision. A clear fact when we consider that no apprentice of any master painter produced a work of comparable vision, such as a second Sistine Chapel. Lowe's obeisance before the clone is inane and idolatrous; it lacks awareness, recognition, or loss of trust in what in fact the sensitive observer witnesses before any work of art.

And that is precisely the measurable, quantifiable difference—the 'aura,' or what is genuine is the idiosyncratic touch of the human hand. The distinctly personal element, which contains the mark of the mind in its every contour, and no clone, however expert, will ever possess that cohesiveness, even when such clones are made not only through technological means that seem infallible and superior but manual ones as well.[7] For this is a matter of imagination, of an original idea born of an original experience, and, as stated, of the uniqueness of the singular object. What determines that is variable, but artistic cohesion is evident to the trained eye and such an eye will recognize that Factum Arte's clones are a combination of both technological and manual functions. However precise their scanners and however high the definition of their printers, what they will betray is the mark of a series of linear, crisscrossing ink jets, not a thinking mind orbiting according to its own logic, and that combined with the manual touch of a restorer who, however expert, leaves its mark too, which is not the mark of Veronese or of Caravaggio. Such artists painted with great velocity and fluidity to render the dynamism of their subjects, but printers cannot replicate the nuances which are the mark of the artist's very character, his or her fingerprints or DNA, nor the particular touch of how each artist physically applies paint to the canvas. In honoring such, we honor the hand of the artist in the *texture* of the work, its surface, tactile façade, or architecture; if that is altered, our intellectual and sensual experience of the

---

7 Prior to the dawn of late 20th century technology, it was the fake, which often involved not copies of specific paintings but paintings in the *style* of a specific artist that led to similar dilemmas. Orson Welles investigates the question of the fake in his arresting film *F for Fake* (Specialty Films, 1973; Criterion 2005). A new documentary on de Hory by Jeff Oppenheimer and Mark Forgy is currently underway. For details: http://www.elmyr.net

work is altered and reduced. And this is to say nothing of the material consistency of such clones. Ergo, all that makes a style is palpably absent.

The other predicament, and one well-rehearsed, is that, once copied, every artwork (save, essentially, the photograph) begins to lose its distinctiveness and that is the serious moral threat. The horror of the mass produced copy is depicted with considerable force in the opening of Jodorowsky's *Holy Mountain*. And for all too many, van Gogh is first encountered as a glossy image on a coffee mug and Beethoven heard as a jaunty jingle in a commercial, or as a cellphone ring. Immuring ourselves against these degradations is almost wholly impossible; likewise, we are so far beyond the threshold that calling for the destruction of the icons would be nothing less than futile, a superficial anarchy that would not ameliorate or address the core of the crisis. While technological devices can register what the human cannot, they can only verify facts, yet art is not in the facts but in the thought, and the aura meter, or whatever other device, cannot think the thought. It just registers what it's been programmed to register; it cannot contemplate or raise questions, just as the scanner and the restorer cannot replicate the mind or the idiosyncratic touch of the artist. For there *is* genius and there *are* hierarchies—Duchamp's touch is not the touch of Leonardo. Even if a Menard can seem to produce "word for word and line for line" the pages of Cervantes, they will never be the pages of Cervantes, only an imitation of the pages of Cervantes. Laughable as it must sound to pronounce—though to the *iconodules* there is no difference—Factum Arte's scanners are not equivalent to the hand of Veronese. And that is not to fetishize Veronese and his achievements but to recognize his utter particularity and the value of the original object, and this is the ethical point—if the material aspect largely can be replicated, it seems necessary to stress anew the menace that such replication poses to the potency of the original. The more copies proliferate, the more that potency is reduced and our aesthetic experience demoralized. Other factors contribute to this demoralization, such as the overcrowding of museums, which have made them less palaces of the muses and silence and more malls and houses of commerce where solitary communion with works of art is near but impossible to obtain. Valéry found the concept of the museum itself the product of an irrational civilization devoid of the taste for pleasure. "Just as a collection of pictures constitutes an abuse of space that does violence to the eyesight, so a close juxtaposition of outstanding works offends the intelligence." Earlier in the same essay he makes an analogy between the juxtaposition of artworks and music and notes how "the ear could not tolerate the sound of ten orchestras at once."[8] But if the difference between an original and a facsimile of Factum Arte's order isn't discernible to the naked eye of most and if some exult over a clone that does not testify to the value or supremacy of the clone, certainly not its authenticity. Exceptional as it may be, an Elmyr de Hory is strictly not a Modigliani. What it instead testifies to is the limits of perception, the failure of feeling, or the devastatingly poor quality of the spectator's degree of cultivation. Or the triumph of the icon. In this, one of the shadows of the demiurge continues to haunt us. The egalitarian view would be to proclaim that the copy democratizes art and makes it available to all, but the only real encounter with a work of art occurs when one encounters it in its original medium. If we are to be truly exacting, and art demands such rigor, we must consider the degree to which art is even

---

8   Paul Valéry, *Degas, Manet, Morisot* (New York: Pantheon Books, 1960), 204, 203. This is Volume XII of *The Collected Works of Paul Valery*, Bollingen Series XLV.

available to us at all and not treat such intractable material as if it is so easily accessible. Blanchot raises this very question when he asserts that *no work*, "be it the most immediately contemporary one, is at our disposal, for we must make ourselves receptive to it. We know that we have almost nothing of the *Iliad* and almost nothing of the *Divine Comedy*. We know that these works, even if they are transmitted without error, escape us and are estranged from us by the reading that makes them accessible to us. Everything separates us from them: the gods, the world, the language, what we know and do not, but above all our knowledge—our knowledge of Homer and our always more precise knowledge of what to attribute to the civilization of Homer. Here, familiarity succeeds only in making the strangeness of books go unnoticed."[9] Although he is commenting on literature, unquestionably, this applies to all art, and his remarks are born of a reflection upon George Duthuit's *Le musée inimaginable: Essai par l'image*, and upon Curtius, who doesn't believe a work of art is even reproducible. If artworks themselves are distant to us, facsimiles are even further afield. That work such as Lowe's threatens to usurp originals in a way hitherto unforeseen should make us wary of how technology aids our ability to deceive and prompt us to become more cultivated, as Tuncel urges in the work before you.

In the mid-60s, before the advent of our current digital technology, Heidegger noted that it "is not that the world is becoming entirely technical which is really uncanny. Far more uncanny is our being unprepared for this transformation, our inability to

---

9 Maurice Blanchot, "Museum Sickness," *Friendship* (California: Stanford University Press, 1997), 42.

confront meditatively what is really dawning in this age."[10] The first epigraph to Debord's *Society of the Spectacle* is Feurbach's observation regarding the preference for the sign over the signified thing, for the copy over the original, of representation to reality, and it is an incisive and unsettling observation that, alarmingly, is increasingly apposite. The *Darstellung* becomes more real to many than what it is a projection of. It is not actual presence, but mediated presence which is often actually preferred, or which seduces us with its entrancing power—hence the hypnotic allure of the screen. Plato's allegory of the cave could not now be more pertinent. The prisoners remain, but the startling difference is that the shadows aren't mistaken for reality; the reflections are clearly recognized as reflections, but the prisoners prefer them … One hears the enslaved declare, "They're *more* real." What we are now in the midst of is a new manifestation of the iconoclast controversy.

Regardless of one's position vis-à-vis the cloning of artworks and the preference of shadows to reality, the process of cloning demands being interrogated, for it raises vexing questions about the nature of our aesthetic experiences that are more than purely aesthetic. Every serious work of art extends beyond the aesthetic domain and is not ever limited to that domain. For all serious art is fundamentally philosophical; in its concern with existence itself, it is ontological, a *thinking* of existence, even if it is 'nihilistic' and questions the validity or value of existence. Eventually such art would have to pursue its instincts to their absolute ends, but that is another matter. While Debord's combative desire to dismantle or annihilate the society of the spectacle is understandable, it is also myopic if not misguided. Based on a circumscribed concep-

---

10 Martin Heidegger, *Discourse on Thinking* (New York: Harper & Row, 1966), 52.

tion of illusion, it limits the morphological character of spectacle and presupposes that illusion is inherently dangerous and spectacle monological. In this way, there is nothing Nietzschean in Debord's desire, or in his understanding of illusion. He is kicking against the pricks. If the *type* of spectacle that Debord critiques is to be abolished, spectacle in and of itself is not. From the cave paintings of Lascaux to multi-media projects like Greenaway's *Leonardo's Last Supper*, the spectacle has been an ever present if not fundamental and intrinsic element of every society, from the archaic to the contemporary. And it will remain so. Spectacle is not something that can be eradicated. The task is not to harm or destroy the society of the spectacle, but to *reconfigure* it and to consider it from alternative perspectives. While Debord rightly lamented the alienation of the spectator for instance, Artaud recognized that problem in the 1930s, but Debord didn't learn from his visionary project, or from his piercing insights and incantatory declarations. Although he may have failed to achieve his visions, Artaud forged clear pathways with them, striving for instance to establish direct and intensified relations between the spectator and the spectacle, to be free for instance of the limit, barrier, and convention of the proscenium arch.

The architecture of a theatre cannot be fixed—a formulaic and structural imposition—but must be constructed according to the particularities of each spectacle. If there are limits to or practical 'flaws' in his proposals, as Rimbaud noted in his *voyant lettre* the failure of the innovator is of no consequence because he has made advancements; other "horrible workers" pick up the arrows where the previous seers have left them and shoot them into new horizons, beginning where the others succumbed. With companies such as the Laboratory of Jerzy Grotowski, Beck and Malina's

Living Theatre, and Mnouchkine's Le Théâtre du Soleil, aspects of Artaud's vision *were* achieved.[11] Their work revealed that renewed forms of spectacle *are* possible. And the renewal of spectacle is but one of the many other urgent questions that Tuncel explores in *Towards a Genealogy of Spectacle*. How a spectacle is created, what it reveals of its epoch, and how every spectator receives it are all elements of the *character* of spectacle that Tuncel believes Debord and other thinkers of the spectacle have not sufficiently tended to. Despite the pervasiveness of spectacle in our culture it remains for Tuncel the least understood phenomenon, even though we are completely immersed in spectacles and even though our very lives are indelibly shaped by spectacular experiences. Tuncel claims that there is little thought in general about the nature and character of spectacle, an omission which has driven him to extract the essential problems ingrained in what he refers to as our *pathos of spectacle*, a concept that recalls Nietzsche's *pathos of distance* and Deleuze's thinking on affect in cinema. Tuncel's concept is broad and not restricted to affect alone as one might presume but concerns not only *how* spectacles are experienced and their historical character, but *what* they impart and say

---

11 Many filmmakers, both in avant-garde and mainstream cinema, also adopted Artaud's principles. Bertolucci's *Partner* (1968) is not only deeply informed by *The Theater and Its Double*, but Giacobbe, the principle character of the film, quotes from Artaud's book in the opening scene. Giacobbe is a theater director striving for revolution. In an interview, Bertolucci discussed the ideal spectator of his film and spoke of the oneiric as a form of action: "The behavior of the spectator of *Partner* should be that of the ideal spectator, i.e., a very passive spectator who succeeds in finding in the one hour and forty-five minutes of the screening enough time to sleep at least ten minutes and during these ten minutes to dream, thus overcoming his own passivity. I think that should be every spectator's normal behavior in the cinema." See Bernardo Bertolucci, *Interviews*, (eds.) Fabien S. Gérard, Thomas Jefferson Kline, Bruce H. Sklarew (Mississippi: University Press of Mississippi, 2000), 38.

of values, how they are in fact interwoven with the established values of a particular culture.

> What I call *pathos of spectacle* is the coalescence of ways of experiencing spectacles, some dominant and widespread, some marginal, within the same historical epoch of a given culture or civilization. In other words, there is a pathos of spectacle that corresponds to a given system of values.

Whenever we encounter this concept then, we must sustain its broad character and its multiple dimensions. Where are we, Tuncel wonders, from an intra-psychic standpoint when we experience spectacle? Is there a pathos of spectacle within a historical and cultural context? If so, of what is it composed? What does each spectacle reveal of the spectacle maker? Too, what does it reveal of our epoch and its crises?

It is precisely through the genealogical method that spectacle as a configuration of inter-related forces can be made transparent, for this method reveals dialectical tensions and confrontations, thereby identifying the field where agonistic values clash and establish institutions or phenomena such as spectacle. Tuncel achieves this transparency through creating a schema of the inner and outer forces that spectacle comprises, with the former including imagination, ecstasy, movement, feeling, psyche, language, etc., and the latter including the spectacle itself, the spectator, and the creator(s) of the spectacle. It is only through such a micro and macro analysis that any diagnosis of this phenomenon can be made, and this involves a historical, aesthetic, sometimes political, and genetic treatment of spectacle. In exploring the genetic history of spectacle though, it is not some essentialist origin that Tuncel is in search of; the genealogical method exposes the humanistic and universalist fallacy of unbroken continuity, thereby revealing the contest of various conflicting forces that strive for domination. One of Tuncel's aims is to establish a sensible inter-relation within a cross-section of spectacles in order to analyze and evaluate how the different forces of spectacle function together, how both the inner and outer layers relate. Through this, he addresses many of the dilemmas that plagued Artaud and Debord: the separation or schism between the spectator and the spectacle, the obstacle of the passive spectator, the invisible or unconscious aspects of spectacle, collective feelings, the collective unconscious, and the quality of imagination. If this however seems like a work addressed only to theorists, it isn't—Tuncel's genealogy is an invitation not only to the thinkers and creators of spectacle, but to inquisitive spectators. Since the artist often advances far beyond the spectator, if spectacle itself is to "soar to new heights" as Tuncel demands it must, that in part requires an ever more cultivated audience and he is keenly sensitive to this necessity, which is why his book also addresses spectacle attendees. Nonetheless, he does not suffer from the all-too prevalent utopic view of democracy that infects our time. His criticism of what he refers to as the nihilistic attitude of the modern era, which believes that every spectacle is open to all, that any person can attend any spectacle, is refreshing and incisive. It is like an elder monk throwing a naive acolyte into frigid water. Concealed in the democratization of spectacle is disregard and disdain if not even contempt for the "cult value" of spectacle. For what is hieratic. Unfortunately, Tuncel never elucidates his own definition of "cult" or of "cult value," but as far as I understand his use of the phrase, and charged as it is it demands explication, he probably intends to evoke the Latin sense of *cultus*, which would be care, labor, and cultivation, or tending—not worship or blind reverence let alone idolatry and the extremist beliefs typically associated with what is cultish. It is also perhaps meant to signify that which is singular and which can only be appreciated by the few, which would be in line with his critical view of utopic democratic principles, and his celebration of what is more exacting and rarefied and what is generally condemned as elitist, obscurantist, or difficult. And the Latin root of *cultus* forms the basis of the word cultivated. Thinkers like Bataille, Blanchot, and Klossowski sought to sustain such values and to honor them through creating secret societies like Acéphale and Collège de Sociologie. Others we're not aware of may exist. And new ones will be formed. For one must ask: *who can live up to the demands of each individual spectacle*? Is, for instance, every spectator capable of living up to Hermann Nitsch's ritualistic events? Or the theatre of Howard Barker? Is not the inattentiveness that certain more exacting work receives a sign that most spectators cannot live up to it? More discerning spectators are aware of these situations; indiscriminate omnivores eat without thought the body of the entire animal. The criticism such spectacles receive is generally more reflective of the *critic's* myopia than of the work itself . . . Aside from our own subjective experience of a spectacle, it is imperative to consider what each artist wants for his or her work of art. "In what spirit," Tuncel asks, "has the spectacle been created? How was it experienced by its maker(s) and the spectators alike?" What is it that the work itself *is*? What is it doing? Have we let it articulate itself in our thought, in our reflections upon it, in our criticism? Have we let it truly infect us? Have we risked *contagion*? The gift of art is to be received with comparable energy, concentration, and intensity. For that to occur, the spectator of an artwork must exert a degree of concentration close to if not equal to that which the artist exerted during the creation of the work. Octavio Paz expressed a similar view of modern poetry when stating that it "demands total surrender (and an equally total vigilance)."[12] Pleasure alone isn't sufficient, but even if one believes it is, pleasure is not a purely automatic or natural aesthetic experience, born of some seemingly primordial or native human trait but is contingent upon how one is cultivated, just as are emotional responses.[13] There is a degree of sacrifice that every spectator must risk before a work of art. Art deserves and demands serious attention and without this devoted surrender of oneself to art, one's experience of it will always be limited. There is fear in such reservation; fear of the loss of self, fear of the ecstatic, fear of real communion with the spectacle. To enter these realms one must cultivate intense states of silence, one must develop incubatory praxes. Such silence is rare in our noisome era—as is *hesychia*—, yet invoking silence is not to call for a sinister form of isola-

---

12 Octavio Paz, *Alternating Current* (New York: Arcade Publishing, 1990), 5.

13 In opposition to the exacting proposal I make some might prefer the Japanese technique of the "first glance," which László Krasznahorkai discusses in "Gone Berserk in Paradise (Notes on the Aesthetics of Total Culture in Japan)." The Japanese posit that no time but the instant of the first glance is necessary for deciphering what one sees. However, this technique is demanding in its own right and seems to require a high degree of cultivation or considerable perceptive acuity, for it is described as "the final phase of time, an unbelievably solid 'point' where time is almost suspended" (sound reminiscent of something?), and although further glances are not necessary for understanding what one sees, this experience also requires an encounter between "the real depth of reality" and the spectator; "it is a direct revelation and amazement of sudden 'understanding'" and is further described as a "transcendent floating that embraces the whole world within a single instance." But is to decipher and understand of primary concern? What of the experience of non-knowledge, and of being catapulted into the vortexes and silences of the enigma? For Krasznahorkai's essay, visit this section of his website: http://www.krasznahorkai.hu/prose.html

tion, but quiet communion with a work. As Simonides said, "the gift of silence is free of peril."

In pursuing such questions, questions which perhaps do not always receive single and definitive answers—rightfully so—but which are approached as riddles to be thought out in different ways, Tuncel seeks to understand the "language" of spectacle. Here, language is meant in its widest sense, that is, it is the *morphological* character of spectacle which is Tuncel's concern. His work is an *Versuch* to understand spectacle itself, in its immanence, and to analyze the pathos of spectacle that corresponds to the spirit of our times, for the pathos of spectacle is ever-shifting and different from epoch to epoch. New genealogies of spectacle will consequently be needed in the future. The spectacle of Christ on the cross was composed of an entirely different pathos than are spectacles of the post-ontotheological age. For with the death of God and "excess revealing itself as truth," two significant epochal shifts are signified in Occidental civilization, and with each new shift, there is a need for a new balance and a new conception of the pathos of spectacle, for with each new epoch there is a new conception of illusion and the character of illusion.

The spectacle of Christ is not to the modern Christian (an oxymoron in itself) what it was to Tertullian. A pathway out of the archaic and primitive has been forged, but all too many wish to remain anachronistic.— Excoriating, but true.— There is a new conception of art as well, for "painting" is not to us what it was to Caravaggio or Giotto, and one cannot speak of "painters" from such widely different epochs in the same terms. With these significant shifts—the death of mimesis for instance—we must then ask, how are images experienced? How are images linked to certain types of symbols? What does the image signify to the new epoch? What illusion? What is an image now? Underlying these questions is the demand that spectators become highly cultivated beings, for those who cannot live up to the spectacle that they attend can harm the collective experience of the spectacle.

Some of Tuncel's questions dovetail with the recent diatribes of Peter Greenaway, who expressed similar concerns when rightfully assailing culture at large for its visual illiteracy and cinema for its being essentially corrupted by text, of not being as intrinsic a medium as he believes it must. The genealogical history of cinema isn't to be found in literature or drama as Greenaway avows, nor is it limited to that of cinema, or its more obvious antecedent, the camera, or the *camera obscura*, but to painting and the use of artificial light in the creation of new images. Hence the dire necessity of understanding the image and the history of the image. Are the painters and other images makers of our day sufficiently knowledgeable in this sense?

To focus on cinema, what makes Pasolini, Bergman, Vláčil, and Tarr superior filmmakers in part is their knowledge of the image, of the history of painting and thus of framing, perspective, and composition; cinema is not of course comprised of only those elements, but they are fundamental to the structure of that art. That Dziga Vertov announced the death of cinema in 1922 for similar reasons, and that Artaud also addressed similar problems in his 1938 manifesto reveals that these remain tenacious dilemmas. In the midst of the digital explosion, archivist Paolo Cherchi Usai published his aphoristic tract *The Death of Cinema: History, Cultural Memory and the Digital Dark Age* in 2001, giving us the first such manifesto of the 21st century.[14] Now, just having crossed

---

14 While Usai traces the roots of cinema to painting just as Greenaway, he traces the roots of the moving image to the *thaumatrope* (1825), the magic

the threshold of 2010 (Arthur C. Clarke's novels on the promises and perils of technology resonate strongly here), that nearly 100 years later these dilemmas persist and have in fact intensified attests to the urgency of a genealogy such as Tuncel's. What they also reveal is the devastating stasis of our epoch. But what many prefer is the narcotic, not thought, or titillation, and it is the kaleidoscopic and blinding blitzkrieg completely lacking in *ciphers* or *zephirum* that has in part led to this paucity of thought.[15] While Debord sought to annihilate the society of the spectacle, Tuncel passionately affirms that culture *needs* illusion and that fulfilling that need is imperative. And it is spectacle which is the most potent and lucid if not 'healthy' form of illusion, for such illusions do not purport to have ontological verity, as does the still pernicious illusion of the demiurge. In this, Tuncel is strictly at odds with Debord and other similar thinkers of spectacle and his Nietzschean heritage is evident, for like Nietzsche he recognizes the multiplistic character of illusion and distinguishes between different *types* of illusion. What is perilous is when illusion is taken for truth, or as something absolute that cannot be questioned, or something sacrosanct that cannot be parodied or satirized. The potency of illusion as configured in spectacle becomes for Tuncel

---

lantern (c. 1650), and Chinese shadow plays (180 B.C.). See Paolo Cherchi Usai, *The Death of Cinema: History, Cultural Memory and the Digital Dark Age* (London: BFI Publishing, 2001), 23. An intriguing film to watch in relation to Usai's tract is Bill Morrison's *Decasia: The State of Decay* (New York: Plexifilm, 2004). I would trace the roots of cinema to the cave paintings of Lascaux, for groups of people sat in the dark *watching* paintings that were illuminated by *flickering* juniper fuses, an effect that we may presume gave the paintings a sense of *kineticism* and *mobility*, making them startlingly cinematic.

15 The *cipher,* or *zephirum,* as developed by Tuncel is the *absence* within an artwork—and this takes various forms—that gives the spectator the freedom to dream, think, meditate, etc. and to further engage with the work while in the midst of it. It is for Tuncel part of the structure and mythos of spectacle.

a question of psychic health. Under optimum circumstances he asserts, "artistic spectacles can help create 'healthy' psyches and psychic balances." Wordsworth expressed an analogous view in his little known and rarely read essay on the beautiful and the sublime, proclaiming that our health is contingent upon "frequent" and "strong experiences" of *both* the sublime and the beautiful; in fact, while our "daily well-being" is more dependent for Wordsworth "upon the love and gentleness" that accompanies beauty, it is impossible, he unequivocally professes, *impossible* for a mind to be in a healthy state without both.[16] The need for illusion and the need to understand the character of illusion is one of the fundamental tasks of our age, the post-Nietzschean era of secularism, the age that is of nihilism, which is face to face with increasing fundamentalisms of every type. We are still at war over the image, and with the murder of Theo van Gogh, we have a modern martyr of the image. Its power remains; its force is palpable.

With the veritable death of myth as a guiding focus, how are the people of the post-ontotheological age to orient themselves? While myth informs our thinking to some degree, we do not live by myths as completely as did the Greeks and Romans. Deleuze posits that literature "is the attempt to interpret, in an ingenious way, the myths we no longer understand, at the moment we no longer understand them, since we no longer know how to dream them or reproduce them."[17] Whether we truly lack this oneiric capacity is questionable; at least one individual may and the power of one

---

16 William Wordsworth, "Appendix III [The Sublime and the Beautiful]" in Vol. II of *The Prose Works of William Wordsworth*, (eds.) W.J.B. Owen and Jane Worthington Smyser (Oxford: Clarendon Press, 1974), 349.

17 Gilles Deleuze, *Desert Islands and Other Texts: 1953-1974* (New York: Semiotext(e), 2004), 12.

as Thoreau attested is potent enough a force to give birth to a lasting transfiguration. Nevertheless, does our current literature adequately interpret misunderstood myths? Does our art? If it doesn't, are the artists of the age ready and willing to destroy existing forms of art in order to create new ones, albeit risking disaster? When urgent questions are raised regarding the status of the book or the painting or other art forms, one often hears the fearful and sacrosanct voices of the all too many who have made art into the new religion—painting is not dead, the book is not dead, etc. There is no crisis; everything is certain. Let us be satisfied and content that we are "artists," that most maligned word. Existence is validated; significance is firmly attested. With this, art becomes dogma. In this, there is a refusal of thought. Yet with the creation of every new work of merit, of those rare works that truly transfigure or break or alter a genre so significantly that returning to the traditional or atypical form is no longer possible, the threat of destruction *is* imminent. Something *has* shattered. In speaking of the possibility of "new gods" (to which I see no necessity whatsoever), "new myths," and "new auras," Tuncel implies that the artists of our epoch are not adequately interpreting myth. Even if one is at odds with some—or many—of his diagnoses—and many artists and spectators *will* be and *will* probably note sufficient counter-examples to the lacunae he avows exist—on a larger scale, thinking historically and epochally, the crises he professes exist *do* in fact exist. If the example of certain individual artists in every field may testify against his view, the work of such artists is surely the result of their asking similar questions and recognizing similar dilemmas, as we see with Greenaway, Barker, Tarr, and others. For Tuncel, this is our crisis: the lack of context, of a mythic dimension of some kind, and of "cult values." Ultimately, his text is a challenge and provocation to both artists *and* spectators—*cultivate a new "cult" value for new art forms and spectacles*. This in part entails developing more cultivated spectators, which comprises not only intellectual cultivation, but the cultivation of the body and the senses, and in the hyper-technological age, of "a gathering of *techne* in a poetic fashion." Operating here are not only questions of value but of affect and power, and as Tuncel points out, problems in the spectacular domain are reproduced in the unconscious of spectators, just as the damaged psyche of the artist can be reproduced in his or her artwork. How much overcoming has been achieved? What has been transfigured? Here we are caught in a vicious labyrinth whose roots stretch back to our not too distant past. In one of his aphorisms, Tuncel notes that in its adoption of Greco-Roman culture, modernity replicated a decayed art form, thereby inheriting the disintegration of art and spectacles in adopting cultures in decline. In this way, we are still Greeks and Romans, perhaps in part dead ones, but also richer, expanded, "Orientalized," technicized (often confused) Greeks and Romans. We still have not learned enough from what Emerson and Nietzsche have said of history. But it is precisely through artistic activity that a revitalization of culture will transpire—when this occurs, Tuncel pronounces, "a new need for grand spectacle presses itself into that culture; it is as though the renewed culture were to desire to see its new shape in the mirror." Although we exist in a time continuum that binds us to the past, every epoch is also a *new* epoch and one that gives birth to a new culture. Thus it is incumbent upon us to shape our future as much as that is possible, to let the imagination give it contour, for no creative energy can die, no *Arkè*: Heraclitean transformation is the Law, but, as Eliot says, "at the still point of the turning world." Do you hear the voices, the ancient voices? Since politicization, moralization, and the gradual popularization of culture have led to the emaciation of poetics, mythology, and ecstasy, spectacle and spectacular experience must free themselves of such elements in order to be transfigured. This is how the *new* pathos of spectacle may emerge and once it begins to emerge, the symbolic spectacle(s) of *our* epoch will be clearer. In *The History of Sexuality* Foucault called for an *ars erotica* and while we are still in need of that, Tuncel urges us to cultivate an *ars ecstasis* and for spectacle, spectacle makers, and spectators in all their manifestations to be ecstatic. It should be evident though that this mode of ecstasy is not limited to one but clearly embodies *two* archetypal "deities" . . . As a young agonist once said, "now follow me to the tragedy and sacrifice along with me in the temple of both deities!"

New York,
7 January 2011

Author's Introduction

§ 1
It has been some time, at least a few years, since I was first intrigued by the question of spectacle. Philosophical literature has not posed sufficient questions in this area and has not shed enough light on this problem, because so much remains in obscurity and so much in fragments. There is one major work in the twentieth century, namely *The Society of the Spectacle* by Guy Debord, which is invoked among the learned each time the subject comes up. However insightful the book may be, its pretension to sell a part as the whole is far from being profound, not to mention the problems of Debord's pessimism. Commodification of spectacle or manifestation of spectacle as mass media in our age is only one aspect of spectacle. Literature on the subject, however, is scattered over many fields and spirits, and it is one of the tasks of this project to bring at least some of the insights on spectacle together.

§ 2
The question that intrigued me regarding spectacle has been: where are we, either as a spectator or as a spectacle maker, when we experience a spectacle? Where are we from the standpoint of our inner lives? Additionally I wondered if there is a *pathos of*

spectacle within a historical and a cultural context, and if so, what does it consist of? Again, within a historical context, are all types of spectacles somehow related to one another? If so, how are they related? What binds them together? I have more questions than answers, and this is why I embarked on this journey of exploring this topic by way of some of the authors who have something to say about it. I simply want to understand the pathos of spectacle of our age; for this reason, I focus on post-Kantian works (with occasional references to classical debates). Despite some insights, I find Debord's starting and ending notes as insufficient, and many academics sing his song when the subject of spectacle comes up.

§ 3
What I call *pathos of spectacle* is the coalescence of ways of experiencing spectacles, some dominant and widespread, some marginal, within the same historical epoch of a given culture or civilization. In other words, there is a pathos of spectacle that corresponds to a given system of values.

§ 4
There are, no doubt, many ways in which spectacle has come to be understood and interpreted. Its Latin root *spectaculis* is a derivative of *spectare* which means 'to watch, to look at.' Its Greek equivalent *theaomai,* from which *theatron* is derived, likewise means 'to view, to observe, to contemplate.' (*Theama,* which means 'sight' and 'spectacle', is also derived from the same verb.) Is spectacle then that which we watch or is it that which a culture considers worthy of viewing collectively? It is necessary to put all these definitions aside during this project although they

are not entirely useless; they may, however, prevent us from a persistent questioning.

§ 5
Spectacular experience is as universal as linguistic experience. This was the case for archaic societies and even more so now than ever. We can speculate that archaic human beings gathered and looked at natural phenomena with amazement and saw spirits in them; this was possibly one of their spectacles. In our age, we are surrounded by the spectacles made by human beings whether these are urban spectacles, mass media, artistic spectacles, spectacles of sport events, or other spectacles. To a large extent these spectacles shape our being.

§ 6
This project is an attempt to understand the inner dynamics or the forces that are at work in our *spectacular experiences* despite the differences in various types of spectacle—one can, for instance, speak of artistic spectacle as well as political spectacle and spectacle of life. Although the same forces can be found in all spectacles, though in different intensities, empowerment, and constellations, our examples will be drawn mostly from artistic spectacles since spectacle is recreated in the artistic domain and since art is the activity of creativity *per se*. The relationship between different types of spectacles in the same world-interpretation may not be apparent *prima facie* since this relationship is not direct; this has to be worked out from bottom up in a larger project.

§ 7
Our study here is sensitive to two historical considerations. First, it is confined to the spectacular experiences that we find in *Occidental* world-interpretation. A study of different ways of experiencing spectacle in other cultural contexts, though outside the scope of this work, can shed light on some of the problems we are faced with in this area. In the internationalized world we live in today, there are hybrid forms of spectacle, cross-breeding of spectacles. In order to understand spectacle, its dynamics and problems, it is important to study the native soil of a spectacular experience; only then can a comparative study of spectacular experiences be fruitful. Second, spectacular experiences, like all other human experiences, belong to their epoch; that is, they bear a close affinity to their age. This affinity works reciprocally in various constellations: they are shaped by the highest values of their age, but they also shape their age.

§ 8
I use the term 'force' in the genealogical sense, that is, in the sense of an event or an activity, which can be analyzed in relation to another force and in a constellation of forces. The multiplicity of forces analyzed as such yields a meaning that is somewhat different from the meaning of the force itself. This also reveals the methodology of the project. The method of genealogy, which was developed first by Nietzsche and later cultivated by Foucault in recent times, is used here to understand spectacle as a configuration of inter-related forces. Genealogy helps pose the question as to the origin of things in their originary constellation.

§ 9

There are two layers in this project: First, the forces that make spectacle happen; namely, the spectacle itself, the spectator(s) and the creator(s) of the spectacle. I call these *the outer forces of spectacle*. Part I of the book deals with this layer. Second, the forces which are at work in spectacle such as imagination, ecstasy, movement, feeling, psyche, language, etc. These I call *the inner forces of spectacle*. Part II of the book deals with these inner forces. Such a division between the inner and the outer, or a two-tiered genealogy, may be considered unnecessary especially when one considers that all forces come together in the experience of spectacle. Since we are operating under the Spectacle/spectacle *coupure* or cut of our age (which will be designated as S/s hereafter), this division has become inevitable.

§ 10

The project does not aim for a completeness of all of the forces of spectacle, but rather a *sensible* inter-relationship within their possible cross-sections. But the challenge of the project is not only to make sense of the working of the forces together within a genealogical layer, but also how the two layers relate to each other so as to explain an important aspect of spectacle. In the appendix to Part II of the book, some ways of correlating the two layers will be worked out.

§ 11

Finally, this project is an invitation to the thinkers and creators of spectacle and the inquisitive spectators to ponder through the problems of spectacle in our age. It does not pretend to give answers or solutions to some of the pervasive and difficult questions in this area. On the contrary, with this project I intend to open up yet another space in which questions can be posed and various issues can be explored. Spectacle is not, by any means, the only human condition. However, it is a significant aspect of human existence and has become more so especially in the age of technological reproduction and mass media and is in a dynamic relationship with other aspects of human existence. Its problems, therefore, affect the collective culture and remain, for those who are concerned, to be addressed.

Part I

Unity of Spectacle:

The Outer Forces of Spectacle

§ 12

By the unity of spectacle what is meant is the coming-together of the following three forces: the creator(s) of spectacle, the spectator(s) and the spectacle itself. There are many ways in which this constellation can take shape, where the roles of each are different, as, for instance, in different cultural or epochal contexts. As soon as a culture creates something and puts it on "stage" for all to view, it has a spectacular experience. On the other hand, one can even imagine a cultural state in which there is no distinction between a spectacle and a spectator, that is, in which the line of separation melts away. However, since the ancient Greeks, especially since the rise of tragic spectacle, this separation cannot be thought away; it has become ingrained into the spectacular experiences of the Occidental world. I will present the unity of spectacle diagrammatically as follows (the problem of the passive spectator lies in this cut):

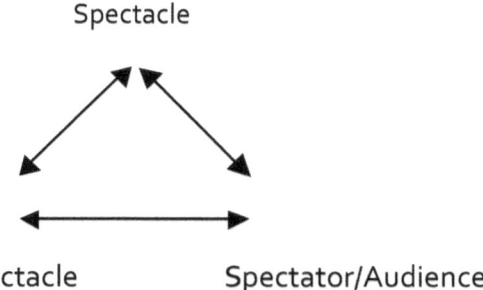

Spectacle

Creator(s) of spectacle   Spectator/Audience

§ 13
For a spectacle to happen, these forces must meet and somehow complement each other. This encounter has both visible and invisible, conscious and unconscious aspects; the latter being harder to detect and its problems harder to address. For example, the collective feelings, the level of imagination, and the collective unconscious belong to this invisible aspect.

§ 14
The diagram above simplifies a complex phenomenon. The complexity lies in the fact that all the forces that make up the unity of spectacle are themselves plural (more than one entity) and multiplistic (more than one force within an entity). How then, in such a diversity of forces, can one speak of unity? What is it that brings these various forces together and how does this happen? Before we explore these questions, we need to examine the forces of spectacle.

§ 15
Spectacle. Anything that is viewed, heard, and experienced collectively. The spectrum for artistic spectacles is broad and includes hybrid forms as well. A spectacle brings together a com-

munity of spectators who are *loosely* or closely associated with one another. What binds the spectators together in a given spectacle will be dealt with later. An artwork that does not come to spectacle is not spectacular; this is brought up to illustrate that a genealogy of spectacle is not the same as a philosophy of art or an aesthetics, although they overlap with one another in many ways.

§ 16
Spectator. From the artist's standpoint, one can speak of the actual spectator who experiences the spectacle, the hyper-spectator who is present spiritually (the material the artist derives from), and the virtual spectator (the artist's expected spectator). In a grand artistic spectacle all three types of spectators coincide; this is, in fact, what makes a spectacle grand insofar as the audience is concerned. From the spectator's standpoint, this has to do with the participation of the spectator, at whatever level and with whatever intensity, physically or inwardly. Audience: Each spectator experiences spectacle ultimately individually; what we call 'audience' is a group of individual spectators, loosely or closely bound together, who experience the same spectacle together. A spectacle without spectator is as absurd as its opposite. In fact, the creators of spectacle derive their source from the hyper-spectator that stands for the pool of images and symbols that are available to the artist. We can call this pool the *collective unconscious* of spectacle.

§ 17
Contrary to the trend of the passive spectator that is dominant in contemporary society, spectators play a significant role in

the making of the *spectacular event* and determine, to some extent, the level of greatness it reaches.

§ 18
Creator of spectacle. Those forces which are directly and/or indirectly involved with the creation of an artistic spectacle, usually designated as artist, poet, curator, playwright, director, singer, dancer, sculptor, painter, composer, conductor, musician, etc. The term 'artist' will be reserved for this function. An artist's world-view and vision play a crucial role in artistic spectacles; the artist, in many ways, is a function of his/her culture, although the artist is the one who is expected to uphold uniqueness and a certain type of individualism. In other words, in an artist, that which is individual and that which is collective are highly intensified and coincide. It is *easy* for an artistically rich culture to produce rich artists, but will also produce poor artists, whereas it may be *difficult* for an artistically poor culture to produce rich artists, but it can do so when the individual artist raises the flag of creation even above the heads of his contemporaries (usually such artists will not be understood by them). An artist's world-view becomes important when the work comes to spectacle since those elements of the world-view that are in the work will have certain *affect* on the audience and the culture. These elements and these affects can impoverish or enrich the culture especially if we keep in mind that spectacles, more specifically artistic spectacles, play a primary role in culture-making.

§ 19
Moreover, the egoism of the modern artist has a debilitating effect on the experience of spectacle—one can infer that such

egoism did not exist in the soul of ancient creators—and may, paradoxically enough, deprive it of being a rich experience. For one thing, it is usually not only the author/composer of a work who makes the spectacular event possible (unless it is a solo performance); for another thing, when a work is presented as a spectacle, it no longer *belongs* to its author but to the community of spectacle (in this sense, to borrow Barthes' phrase, the author is dead, what we are left with is this community).

§ 20

When artistic spectacles enter into competition (or if there is a competition in a particular spectacle), the judges of spectacle also appear as the outer forces of spectacle that determine the highest and the best spectacle according to the rules of the contest in question. This is how the best tragedies were determined in ancient Greece. To understand the role of the "agondikasts" (the judges of contest), one needs to understand the inner dynamics, the spirit of competition among the agonistic Greeks. Today's competitions are agonistic on the surface, but do not carry the spirit of agon itself (simply said, we do not live in an agonal age).

§ 21

Societies function with hierarchies although what determines them varies (sometimes even hierarchies are denied to exist, but this is only a presumption). However, hierarchies, whether embodied in ruling values or ruling human beings, are always there. The central question is as to the nature of the prevailing hierarchy. The question of hierarchy also applies to spectacular relations. Spectacle-makers must recognize a hierarchy among all artistic spectacles in their own cultural context and, moreover, spectators must be hierarchically situated according to the inner dynamics and demands of the spectacular forces in a given spectacle. This is not to say that hierarchies are fixed, unchanging, and imposed from above. For one thing, there are different types of artistic spectacles demanding their own specific hierarchies. And cultivation is not a static process. Spectacular hierarchies will be formed *naturally* and according to their cult values.

§ 22

The unity of spectacle: the creator, the spectacle, and the spectator(s). What binds spectacle together is one of the most difficult questions to deal with, since there are different principles at work in different spectacles. The question for a mythic age would have been easier to handle: the legends and the sagas about gods and heroes that everyone knew were the binding elements as in the tragic spectacle of ancient Greeks. The epos was, however, the material of the unity (or the semantics of the *language* of spectacle) whereas the symbolic unity (the syntax) consisted of the players of the game as it is in contemporary experience of spectacle (the roles and dispositions of the players being different). Players and pieces complement one another like in a jigsaw puzzle, forming an immanent unity of spectacular forces. Before spectators were amazed at the sight of the sufferings and conflicts of gods and heroes, *techne* was the vessel through which such dramatic presentations could be possible. In our age, however, this amazement has shifted towards technology, technological tools and sight and sound effects; now human beings are amazed only or mostly at their own technological creations. This central problem, no doubt not unique to spectacular experiences, is yet another difficult problem to deal with. We can say at the outset that the forces of spectacle belong together both mythically and historically.

§ 23

The unity of spectacle rises as a whole and falls as a whole, although this may not be apparent *prime facie*; and this may not be so in the short run. For an artist or an artistic spectacle to soar to new heights, its audience must be cultivated, in general, for all spectacles, but in particular for that type of spectacle. Now artistic spectacles themselves may or do play a role in the cultivation of spectators, but they may not be sufficient for that role. Here the necessity of artistic and spectacular *education* comes to the foreground. It often happens that the artists run ahead with their innovations, new styles and creations, leaving the spectatorship behind. If the spectatorship does not rise with the artist and the new spectacle, this will eventually lead to the poverty of spectacular experiences and also to the poverty of arts and spectacles.

§ 24

Every spectacle has a specific audience that fits into it like a lid that matches only its specific pot. Not every spectacle is for everyone; this may sound like an obvious insight, but our technological age, with its disregard for the cult value of spectacle, has created havoc with it and cultivated the nihilistic attitude of "any spectacle for anyone." What makes a specific body of spectators attend a specific spectacle that is uniquely for it can be understood only with the analogy of cult and cult members.[1] In the age of self-entitlement where most do not know their place or power, this problem in spectacular relations has been exacerbated.

§ 25
The unity of spectacle is re-created in different ways in different types of artistic spectacles; the artistic medium determines, to a large extent, how the spectators establish their relationship to the spectacle and its makers.

§ 26
When I say 'unity of spectacle,' I mean an *agonistic* unity and, by no means intend to reduce the singularity and the unique role of each player of the spectacular game to one another. They all have their own place and function and come together for a spectacular event in a given, singular spectacle. To say that the spectator has no role in the spectacle or in its making is as absurd as to say that spectacle is made entirely and only for the audience. Both the classical (that creates a metaphysical separation between the artist and the non-artist) and the popular conceptions of spectacle (that sings the song of "everything is for the people") betray its *eidos* and its unique place in culture and culture making.

§ 27
Most thinkers since Kant, who had things to say on spectacle, have kept the singular aspect of aesthetic experience and, therefore, that of artistic spectacle. In Kant one sees this in his notion of aesthetic judgment, in Nietzsche in the Apollonian, in Foucault in the notion of similitude, and in Barthes in *punctum*. Kant states that one can only say 'this is beautiful,' referring to some one

aesthetic object, but not that all such objects are beautiful. Aesthetic experiences, though universal, are not logically or conceptually bound. What is beautiful is beautiful only to me as an aesthete. Therefore, aesthetic judgments are singular, and through them we manifest our singular existence. For Nietzsche, individual spectators find their *justification* in appearances that are presented to them in artistic spectacles (more specifically in tragedies) just as they are *justified* in their dreams doubly. This artistic justification takes place at the level of the individual since each individual is a unique dreamer and has a unique arsenal of images. Foucault opposes the idea of representation (within the context of painting), that is, creation of copies based on a true model, with his notion of similitude, which ties a variety of singular objects and signs in a series that can go in any direction. Even the singular spectator can be inscribed into the series in a given spectacle. Finally, Barthes claims that it is the *punctum* that pricks the attention of the individual spectator in a photographic spectacle; the *punctum* can be a detail, a coincidence, a trigger for the imagination of the spectator, as opposed to the general information that photos convey, what Barthes calls *studium*. To conclude, it can be said that in a given spectacle a singular spectacle meets singular spectators; whether spectators live up to their singularity in any sense is another matter.

§ 28

In addition to the problem of nihilism (the attitude that says "anything goes" or "anyone can attend any spectacle"), we are faced with the problem of the old morality that reduces all spectacular functions to either morality (à la exoteric Plato), to religion (à la Early Church Fathers), or to education (this became widespread in the modern age). Spectacle must be *liberated* from such moralistic/nihilistic (and utilitarian) reductionisms.

§ 29
The unity of spectacle may evoke Wagner's idea of total artwork. Although there may be overlaps between the two, they are not the same. To see the relationship between the unity of spectacle as presented in this work and the idea of total artwork, it is necessary to examine the three versions of this idea as presented by Wagner in his aesthetic writings and to respond critically to each of them from the standpoint of our genealogy of spectacle (see Part III).

§ 30
For every spectacle, a spectacle-maker who is involved in its making and who is sensitive to the question of spectacle, would ask the following questions: In what spirit has the spectacle been created? How was it experienced by the makers and the spectators alike (in what communal spirit)?

§ 31
The basic task, the challenge in front of us, is to make an attempt to understand the *language* of spectacle, that is, to understand spectacle in itself, in its immanence, and to be able to analyze the pathos of spectacle that corresponds to the spirit of our times.

Part II

The Inner Forces of Spectacle

Chapter 1: Ecstasy

§ 32
Ecstasy, defined broadly, is the universal oneness of all and can be called 'cosmic ecstasy.' Human life is a part of the cosmic cycle and as such has raw ecstasy within itself. To create outlets, cultural formations, for such ecstatic energies and to cultivate oneself as an ecstatic being fall within the realm of ecstatic experiences. We can all be said to be ecstatic in the former sense, but not in the latter sense. To be ecstatic in this latter sense, it is necessary to have created ecstatic formations in culture in which members of that culture cultivate themselves as ecstatic beings. This distinction is made by Nietzsche in *The Birth of Tragedy* when he speaks of the Dionysian barbaric and the Dionysian Greek.

§ 33
If the death of God signifies an epochal turning point in Occidental civilization, the announcement Nietzsche makes in *The Birth of Tragedy* that "excess revealed itself as truth" signifies a shift in spectacular experiences. Excess, that is, the Dionysian, is now as important as the Apollinian, and the Dionysian forces and art impulses play as significant a role as those of the Apollinian. These insights now interject themselves into the epoch-making.

§ 34
Ek-stasis, in its etymological sense, is coming out of oneself or the "loss" of oneself. Now the ultimate loss is one's own death, but in the course of one's life, one can experience ecstatic moments as one comes out of one's everyday-ordinary way of life. Here a distinction can be made regarding general or total ecstasy (what mystics experience, for instance) and particular forms of ecstasy, which cultivate ecstasy in some aspect of human existence. Dance is an ecstasy out of regular movements of the body as in walking, poetry is ecstasy out of everyday language. Orgy or any non-purposeful sexuality is ecstasy in the domain of sexuality in relation to procreative sexuality.

§ 35
Ecstasy, moreover, is to be able to see oneself in the other. In our age, there are many ideologies, systems of bias and bigotry, which are obstacles before such universal ecstasy. But ecstasy, in a deeper sense, is the ability to see oneself in any other creature of this universe without the imposition of everyday ideologies.

§ 36
Ecstatic states, in which one loses oneself with others before a great work of art and its spectacle, can lead to deep and intense emotions and open up wounds in the unconsciousness of the spectators. This could be the cure for one of the curses of our age: superficiality.

§ 37
Why the modern age is less ecstatic (that is why it invests less in ecstatic forms) is explained in different ways by different au-

thors. Nietzsche traces it back to the Socratic rationalism and sees its influence on modernity in the form of Alexandrian culture. Whereas for Bataille, the modern age lost the experience of the sacred and sacrifice[1] in and through which ecstasy can be *communicated*.

§ 38
One of the objections made to ecstasy by those who neither feel nor understand it is that political groups use ecstatic feelings of the masses to excite them for their own ideological agenda. This is, no doubt, an abuse of ecstasy but, by itself, is no objection to the value of ecstasy for culture and its individual members. Furthermore, it is yet another reminder for the importance of unity of culture, that is, that different values somehow belong together forming their own constellations.

§ 39
Spectacle has an ecstatic dimension insofar as it brings all the spectators and spectacle-makers together in one form of unity or another. This coming-together is, by no means, an objection to the singularly diverse community that is the audience, which is rather a loosely associated group held together through a work of art in artistic spectacle.

§ 40
Ecstasy entails, first and foremost, the ecstasy of human beings; one can start from oneself, from one's own species, and then proceed to other beings of this universe. There are artistic

---

1 In the contemporary scene, these dimensions of spectacle are present in Hermann Nitsch's festive theater.

formations that are closer to such ecstatic experiences with human presence than others. Theater is such a formation since it brings human presence on stage and also gathers together various aspects of human existence, such as sound, image and body-movement, under an artistic unity.

§ 41

The problematic or unexamined terms used today like interactivity or participation are different ways of expressing ecstatic unity or, worse, yearnings for such ecstatic experiences that one cannot attain due to epochal difficulties; one such difficulty is the modern obsession with individuality, or what I call pseudo-individuality. The ecstatic unity, on the other hand, does not strip away the individual uniqueness of the participant; on the contrary, it enriches it. Nor are the artists reduced to the state of a spectator. Each force is symbolically necessary for the place it takes up in the experience of spectacle.

§ 42

The ecstatic core of the spectacle is created and sustained by its most ecstatic elements such as music, dance, and song. This function, according to Nietzsche, was fulfilled by the chorus[2] in Greek theater and, if compromised, would lose its force and fabric. This is why he is opposed to A. Schlegel's idea of chorus[2] as "ideal spectator": the ecstatic function of the chorus cannot be reduced to the less ecstatic spectator. Nietzsche, on the other

---

2   I am grateful to Mnouchkin and her theater Theater du Soleil for bringing the Greek theater to a lively presence before a contemporary audience. The performances of *Oresteia* with live music, chorus, dance, and masks that I saw in New York in 1992 were the closest approximation to the Greek tragic performances as I have imagined them to be.

hand, favors Schiller's idea of chorus[3] as the domain of poetic freedom. Here what is at stake is not who the spectator is but rather the elevated, ecstatic high ground of the chorus and its sustenance.

§ 43
One type of chorus in Greek tragedy is the satyr chorus. Satyrs,[3] half-human, half-animal mythic figures associated with the cult of Dionysus, helped create the ecstatic mood for the tragic spectacle. While symbolizing the sexual nature of both men and animals alike, they created an ecstatic bridge between the *civilized* human and *nature*, and hence it was the symbolic expression of Greek *physis* on stage. Modern classical theater, on the other hand, is too clean, too orderly, too *civilized* in contrast to the Greek theater.

§ 44
In addition to the chorus, ancient Greek theater used other techniques to help create the ecstatic mood for the spectacle. One such common technique was the use of the masks that not only facilitated the actor in molding himself into a variety of characters depending on the mask used, but also created a distance between himself and the audience that is needed for the ecstatic leap. Now the ecstasies of the chorus in music, dance, and song are conjoined with the ecstasy in acting. As a result, sounds, movements, lyrics, and character-play meet at an elevated level.

---

3 The experimental theater of Robert Lepage, Ex Machina, uses satyr-like figures on stage symbolically similar to their use in ancient Greek tragedies.

§ 45
The absence of chorus and, consequently of song, dance, and music, in modern theater is one of the symptoms of the disenfranchisement of arts and culture in the modern age. Such an absence may not be a problem for a culture if total artworks also exist in that culture.[4]

§ 46
As was said earlier, ecstasy is also about death. Throughout the course of one's life, one can be *in communication* with death and with the dead in ecstatic states. Such a connection would cultivate a sense of mortality[4] on the part of the spectator. When Barthes talks about death as the *noeme* of photography, he probably has something of this sort in mind; photography too creates a sense of mortality by joining the dead with the living (all art forms revolve around absence and make that which is absent present in their respective medium).

§ 47
In ancient times people invented all kinds of illusions so that they could be in touch with the dead, more specifically the dead to whom they had close ties (family members, spiritual leaders, poets, heroes, etc.). Belief in after-life, heaven/hell, Hades, burial customs are all manifestations of this illusion.

---

[4] There is perhaps nothing as unnerving for a modern person as a public spectacle of death. The death of a matador in a bullfight, the public torture of a criminal to death as practiced in Europe and elsewhere until the end of the eighteenth century, Roman gladiator fights and animal fights, and the Meso-American games in which the members of the losing team were sacrificed to the gods. The historical and cultural context must, undoubtedly, be kept in mind for all of these examples.

§ 48
Burial customs and grave/cemetery designs (when applicable) reflect how human-beings, in a given cultural context, relate to death. Whether it is with the Egyptian pyramids, Lycian rock tombs, Greco-Roman sarcophagus, the dead present themselves in spectacles of death to the living. A more concrete example of such spectacles can be found in the cemeteries of Paris that resemble art galleries in open space.

§ 49
Another type of spectacle of death is the spectacle of war. We are drawn to such spectacles because the cycle of destruction passes through all of us; death is tempting and uncanny. Unlike in the artistic spectacles of death or as in tragic spectacles, in which the sufferings of heroes on stage are closely bound with the sufferings of the spectators, in the spectacles of war in our days (especially as portrayed by the mass media) the sufferings of people are not our sufferings (we are far removed from these sufferings). That is partially why politicians can constantly wage such wars on others with almost no impunity. In short, moderns have lost a primordial sense of mortality (this is parallel to the fact that moderns are also unecstatic).

§ 50
The other dimension of ecstasy is transgression. If the world of taboo, the orderly world, is one half of human life, the other half is the world of transgression where these taboos are violated. Festivals in archaic societies, according to Bataille, fulfilled that rudimentary need for transgression. Within the context of sacrifice, Bataille explains festivals as celebrations of the sacred;

it is "the place and the time of a spectacular letting loose."[5] This letting loose had its limits, its own domain bound by the sacred. In a deeper sense, the festival is not a complete (or a permanent) suspension of the world of taboo, but a negation of it within a 'confined' space. We can also understand the originary world of Greek theater as the world of festivals in, at least, two areas: the link between theater and the revelries of the cult of Dionysus and the festive character[6] of the staging of plays in ancient Greek culture. In addition, the fact that tragic heroes[7] are transgressive types reinforces the transgressive nature of the tragic spectacle. We can then conclude that transgression lies at the genealogical origin of spectacle.

Chapter 2: Illusion, Image, and Symbol

§ 51
Under the heading of illusion, various themes will be brought together: artifice, deception, fantasy, magic and myth. We no longer live in a strictly mythic age, but we can learn from the mythic ages of the past. The fact that there are problematic myths is no objection to the value of the wisdom of ancient myths. To value illusion as illusion, to create an inner psychic balance, to create associations between images and symbols, to raise such associations to the level of collective unconscious, to cultivate story-telling and so on. These are some vital signs for any artistic spectacle.

§ 52
A spectacle lives and makes live illusion as illusion by going straight into the archaic core of illusion-making, that is, the domain of metaphor. Here the nerve-stimuli, sounds, and images are re-arranged in newer constellations,[8] analogous to dream states and functions.

§ 53
Illusion usually carries an imaginary connotation when, for instance, it is associated with fantasy or imago, an image or an appearance. These images can be dream images or images of external reality, however problematic this distinction may be from the standpoint of artistic spectacle. What is of importance for spectacle is two-fold: how these images are experienced, that is,

the imagistic experience, and how these images are linked to certain types of symbols.

§ 54
Images, such as pleasurable illusions, produce a variety of feelings and sensations in the human psyche. It is important to take into account the symbolic aspect of these illusions as well.

§ 55
The debate between the imagists and the symbolists takes on different forms in different historical eras. In the middle ages, it turned into a deadly war between the image-worshippers and the iconoclasts, especially in the Byzantium Empire, when the iconoclasts gained a momentum with the rise of Islam in 7th century A.D. Byzantine royal families, military leaders, and priests were split over this issue and were in such a deadly war that moderate Emperors saw it as the chief problem of the Empire that had to be solved urgently. This conflict is of a tragic order: it is a conflict between the Judaeo-Islamic position which claims that God cannot be reduced to an image, a figure, let alone a human figure, because this will betray His Divine predicate, and the Greco-Roman pagan position that believes in imagistic, figurative representation of gods even in forms (apart from the fact that gods are anthropomorphic, what we have here is the deification of images in general, hence a justification of images in the highest sense). What is needed is the tragic sustenance of the symbolic and the imagistic in their authentic functions, which, according to Nietzsche, exists in early mythic Greek theater.

§ 56
It is in the relationship between imagery and symbolism that the strictly imagistic understanding of illusion becomes insufficient. Symbols, in the realm of image, are not images *per se*, they are rather how the images are thrown in together, which signifies the relationship between them. This includes a host of issues such as a simple relationship between images, the life and death of an image and the movement of images. Can one also speak of relationship between symbols?

§ 57
Symbol, therefore, cannot be understood strictly as non-imagistic, as sound, for instance. However closer the symbol may be to the realm of the invisible, it pertains equally to image and sound. Symbol is the way images and sounds are thrown in together. Both are vital elements of spectacle; impoverishment of one may result in impoverishment of the other.

§ 58
The symbolists of the nineteenth century brought forth what was already an essential aspect of the mythic theater; namely, the poetic aspect of drama, the approximation of drama to the inner states of the soul, the mystery of drama, simplicity of the stage, and theater as the synthesis of all arts. With their move towards symbolism of myth, mystery, and dream-like states, the symbolists made a significant contribution to the pathos of spectacle of our age.

§ 59

The relationship between the imagistic and the symbolic is exemplified in myths, in the image-symbol associations of the stories of gods and heroes. It is these associations that are brought forth in Nietzsche's interpretation of Greek tragedy as the union of the Apollonian and the Dionysian. Their ramifications are far-reaching since they are rooted in the depth of the soul of culture. Pleasurable illusions and symbols of suffering (and compassion), the individual and his/her mortality and belonging are some of these associations. When Nietzsche speaks of Oedipus and Prometheus as the various masks of the suffering Dionysus through the illusory outlet of Apollonian imagery, when he speaks of the chorus of satyrs—the satyr as the sacred animal that stands for such a mythic association—these are all examples for the union of images and symbols in a sacred context. Tragedy sits on the invisible terrain of mythology and recreates it as yet another layer.

§ 60

These associations do not fit into the nineteenth-century debate as to whether art is for people or art is for art's sake. These questions were already posed as puzzles in antiquity: art has an immediate, but indirect, relationship to culture. It has its own poetic domain in which it strives for perfection in creativity, but is in contact with other forces of culture from which it derives its vitality. In this way the folk legends, myths, dance, poems and songs form the background, the pool so to speak, based on which the tragic poets strove and competed with each other for greatness in art. And their achievements were recognized and respected as the gems of their culture.

§ 61

Furthermore, these associations do not carry the charge of sacred transgression against art as a stigma since Greek art and mythology, according to Nietzsche, allowed such transgressions as long as they were anchored in a deeper cosmology (the Moira sitting on the throne of all gods and mortals alike), as is exemplified in the myth of Prometheus. To re-create something new, something different, the creator had to commit an act of sacrilege; this is the wisdom of transgression that was also seen in tragic spectacles. Anything that is new, a new creation, is a violation of the old. Renewal of oneself, of culture, of arts, and of society presupposes and demands such transgressions. And mythic spectacles present the appropriate context of transgression.

§ 62

Art is fiction and in artistic spectacles we experience fiction as fiction.[5] They are re-constructed realities that appeal to that which is fictional, fantastic in human life. In artistic spectacles we bring that fictional part of ourselves onto the public arena and experience it collectively. Human beings, among other things, are dreaming, fantastic beings; the presence of fictional beings and props in spectacle appeals to that which is fictional in us.

---

5 Film is a powerful illusion-maker because it approximates life and action like theater, uses moving images (unlike static arts), and is flexible to enter into many different molds according to the vision of the director. For an illusion to take hold of the spectator, it is not sufficient to make the imagery as fantastic as possible, but also to prepare the spectator for an ecstatic mood. Once elevated, the spectator falls into the chasm of the illusion created by the differential between the fantastic and the real.

§ 63
Spectacle is a type of simulation, and also a dissimulation, that a culture needs to fulfill its needs for illusion (under which falls magic, miracle, myths, and so on); it is analogous to what the dream is to the individual dreamer. All that we have in spectacles are simulacra; therefore, all spectacles in a specific socio-cultural, historical context may be related to one another as though in a series and are not copies of an original, transcendental model.

§ 64
According to Klossowski, "simulacrum in its *imitative* sense is the actualization of something incommunicable in itself or of the irrepresentable: properly the phantasm in its obsessional constraint."[9] Therefore, far from being representational as classical thought had conceived it since, at least, Aristotle and his theory of mimesis, a spectacle is about simulacra. It is an attempt to exorcise this obsession by way of simulation. A spectacle makes present that which cannot be shown according to the stereotype or the social censure, and it does so by way of a phantasm that overlays itself over the myth, the source of the myth, and the spectator. Thereby the spectacle *repeats* itself within its own medium and in the spectators, forming a series of simulacra within a spectacular event. Although the simulacrum presupposes the rule of the prevailing stereotype, in spectacle it destroys it. Finally, Klossowski illustrates the spatial presence of simulacra in his fictional works, as, for instance, in *Diana at her Bath*.

§ 65
On the other hand, the theory of simulacrum takes into account, by way of the notion of demonic, the non-rational forces,

what Nietzsche calls 'Dionysian' in an overarching way (which would be id in Freud). Simulacrum, as the field of the life of phantasms and impulses, cannot be understood within the limits of everyday communication, since "singular experience is ...incommunicable and inexchangeable..." It rather exceeds the limits of such communication and lays itself over the collective unconscious. "Beyond the discursive communication, simulacrum creates the conditions of another *communication*, an oblique *communication*, a communication by silence."[10] What is here called 'silence,' can be the collective unconscious, although they are not the same. One can nonetheless speak specifically of silence regarding its role in artistic and spectacular experiences.

§ 66

For his notion of the demonic, Klossowski was influenced by medieval theologians like Tertullian and his studies on Gide and his dialogues with his interrogators. The demon is, according to Tertullian's demonology, "... essentially the simulator and gives form to desires in dreams and spectacles ... and simulates the dead."[11] According to Klossowski, since the demonic spirit does not have being and personality, it must borrow a being other than its own and is prior to every inclination and influence. Feigning nonexistence is the height of the simulacrum of the demon. Art is a simulacrum and the artist a simulator. Moreover, the demon is an autonomous power that operates in every creation, in every spontaneous act and requires a reciprocal act from us. In contrast to the early Christian doctrine of the demonic, Gide "... affirms the Devil's reality as that of a being, not that of a simple principle."[12] In a way, while accepting the Christian tradition of the demonic, Gide inverts it; he affirms the demon as a positive power and gives it a higher role, almost echoing a Zarathustrean or a Manichean position, a position that was rebuked by the Early Church Fathers, most notably, by Augustine. Consequently, for Klossowski the demon is that force which receives and gives form and at the same time provokes desire; it is the force behind the production of simulacra.

§ 67

If there is any "coherence" in a work of art, it must be sought below the level of consciousness: "In order to exercise its constraint, the simulacrum must correspond to the necessity of the phantasm. If the impulse already 'interprets' something for itself, the phantasm remains unintelligible, below the level of consciousness: it is merely the intellect's *ossified incomprehension* of a *state of life*. Because of this, the intellect once again represents the most malicious caricature of 'unreason,' that is, a caricature of the life of the impulses; moreover, the intellect deforms what the phantasm wants to 'say.'"[13] As Klossowski suggests in this passage, the phantasm is deeply rooted in the unconscious and operates according to the life of drives, instincts, and impulses. The intellect, insofar as it operates with concepts that are worn out, cannot *comprehend* such a state of life, but when it does try to comprehend, it deforms the phantasm, that is to say, what the life forces stand for. According to this paradigm, an artwork is an expression of the inner states of its creator and must be approached as such. The spectator too is bound to open up his or her inner states before the work of art so that it can un-conceal itself and create a bond of authenticity through an artistic medium. This is one common thread in post-classical art since impressionism.

§ 68
The intensity of the affect of an illusion depends on the strength of the collective myth that pertains to that illusion. If (and since) we have a collective myth about romantic love, then certain illusions about it may (and will usually) affect us deeply. Unlike in Greek and Roman drama, romantic love as a subject-matter occupies a significant space in modern arts and artistic spectacles.

§ 69
Spectacle does not represent something that is outside the spectacle itself, but is an event as a unique occurrence in time and space. This does not mean, however, that spectacle is not related to other forces of culture, especially those forces that are adjacent to it. It brings to presence, but this bringing-to-presence must be understood within the context of spectacle and its constituent forces. Whether understood as representation of reality or representation (*mimesis*) of action (that Aristotle develops in relation to tragedy), the theory of representation has very little use when it comes to the question of spectacle. Such a theory detaches a human function, namely that of spectacle, from human life or life itself.

§ 70
Magic and miracle have appealed to humans since time immemorial. They both betray the reality principle and reveal something uncanny about existence, they blur the distinction between what is real and what is fantastic, they show the overhumanly in the human, and finally they have been "tools" in the hands of the magic- and miracle-makers to exert power over

their audience. The prominent questions here are: what kinds of magic and miracle exist? And how are they imprinted on culture? The spectacular domain in the West has been usurped by the moralist and the saint via magic and miracle, and modernity has been unable to overturn this usurpation (either perpetuates this usurpation or suffers from a reaction to it).

Chapter 3: Imagination

§ 71

The role of Imagination in aesthetic experience has come to preeminence since Kant's *Critique of Judgment*. This preeminence, though important in many ways, is still subject to criticism; on the one hand, Kant salvages Imagination from the hegemony of the intellect (the most cognitive part of the human mind), on the other hand, he detaches Imagination from the other forces that are at work in the experience of an artistic spectacle. The notion of disinterestedness, therefore, functions like a double-edged sword. Imagination now can protect itself from the imposition of the intellect, but it can also push away other forces that it needs for its richness and vitality. Nietzsche's critique of Kant's disinterestedness hits the mark (how can the Imagination function if the spectator is *unecstatic*, for instance?) and, at the same time, does not hit the mark: how can Imagination function if it does not have its own domain and freedom in relation to Reason and Understanding?

§ 72

Although Kant understood aesthetic experiences as those of the beautiful and the sublime, thus prefiguring Nietzsche's notions of Apollonian and Dionysian, he could not see that the experiences of both the beautiful and the sublime can co-exist in the same artistic experience and the same artistic spectacle.

§ 73

Kant sought the universality of aesthetic experience in the free play of the Imagination either with Understanding or with Reason. Although, for a genealogist, seeking universality is not desirable since the historical determinants cannot be dismissed, something similar to Kantian universality in the realm of spectacle would be the universality of the inner forces of spectacle and their agonistic sustenance. Regarding the outer forces, seeking such a universality would be even more difficult since the S/s cut is analogous to the Subject/object relationship of the Indo-European linguistic structures (spectacle being the active Subject affecting or doing, the spectator as the passive object).

§ 74

Kant demonstrated both the significance of Imagination for human experiences and its limitation as a faculty of presentation. Imagination must stop trying to present that which is great and look within; in this playful mode with Reason and its laws, it enters into the experience of the sublime.

§ 75

Imagination can be understood in the sense of conscious or unconscious imagination. The former is Kant's use of imagination as a faculty of the mind; the latter is dreaming.

§ 76

If unconscious imagination or dreaming is a movement and a transmutation of images within the soul, one can also speak of the movement of other types of sense-data in the body and/or soul. There are no specific terms to explain such movements.

Moreover, different types of sense-data can be conjoined in different combinations. All of these point not only to the limitation of language, but also to the limitation to understand spectacular experiences and their sensual components.

§ 77
For imagination to be rich and active, there has to be, at least, two conditions: one must have high regard for imagination and its activities, and there has to be material (the imagined) for it to work with (myths provide such a rich background for imagination). Usually, in a given system of values, they grow together.

§ 78
Each artistic medium activates and provokes the imagination in different ways that are appropriate to each medium. In hybrid mediums the *affects* are also hybrid.

§ 79
Imagination plays a significant role in the making of the individual since imagination runs wild on its own unique path. This is similar to the path of insightfulness.

Chapter 4: Myth and Aura

§ 80
When scholars and artists since Nietzsche emphasize the cult origin of theater, they are not merely highlighting the historical origin of theater, but its genealogical origin. The historical origin, though useful for a scholarly understanding of spectacle, is less important than the genealogical origin of theater from a spectacular perspective. Genealogical analysis is done not for scholarship alone, but with a sensitivity to the problems in spectacular experiences.

§ 81
Myths bind a people together through their shared fantastic legends and sagas about heroes and gods. In artistic spectacles, the artist recreates these myths, which, in turn, are reinscribed into the soul of the people. Hence the spectacle stands in the middle of the cycle between art and culture, while myths function as the transfiguring mirror.

§ 82
A myth can be told, poetized, drawn, painted, sculpted, sung, composed for music, danced to, performed to, and now even filmed. As such a myth is the bone and the flesh of a work that can hold all artistic expressions together. In short, a myth has a *sympheric* function.

§ 83
There is much confusion as to what myths signify in our age, which is due to the meanings that have been attributed to the

term 'myth.' This has led to the oblivion of the already disfigured mythic experience. On the other hand, the archaic experience of myth was based on the collective experience of stories told about gods and heroes, that is, the shared illusions of a people who looked up to these mythic figures. There was something elevating, something sublime, in the mythic experience.

§ 84

The same myths can be presented in and through different artistic media, and these presentations need to be understood according to the inner dynamics and principles of their corresponding arts forms. Lessing argued for this point in his *Laocoön*, namely, that the story of Laocoön has been presented in poetry (i.e. musical arts) and in painting (i.e. visual/plastic arts) and that one is no more important than the other. They need to be understood in themselves, have their own limits (limited by their nature), and play off one another around these limits. We can expand on Lessing's point and state that the same story can be used in different types of artistic spectacles. From a spectacular standpoint, it is necessary to experience an artistic spectacle from within its own *language* and not approach another artistic spectacle that uses the same theme with the same language.

§ 85

The intimate connection between artistic spectacle and myth has been severed in the modern age, and this severance has to do not only with arts, but, more importantly, with epochal issues, one of which is the disintegration of culture and human experiences (one of the meanings of the death of God). Now myths, in the strict sense, no longer have any vitality in the modern age.[14]

Benjamin explains this severance within the context of mechanical reproduction, as he calls it the loss of the aura of the artwork. This is another way of saying that God is dead, but this does not mean that new gods, new myths, new auras will not be born. Benjamin's critical comments on the arts of mechanical reproduction, more specifically photography and cinema, must be understood as a warning signal as to where these art forms can take us: we can sink in the loss of the aura or we can re-create new traditions, new auras, new cult values within the art forms of mechanical reproduction.

§ 86

Ironically, in his book *On Spectacle*, Tertullian emphasizes the unity of spectacle and myth, as he condemns the artistic and other spectacles of the pagan Romans. Although his condemnations are hardly supportable in this spectacular age, they are revelatory. Yes, we cannot forget the epochal shift of which Tertullian's text is symbolic, and the pathos of spectacle that it represents. However, it reveals that artistic spectacles cannot be detached from their mythic/cult origin, and one cannot give up the pathos of spectacle. After a series of condemnations of everything that is pagan, Tertullian screams: "But now, if you think we are to pass this interval of life here in delights, why are you so ungrateful as not to find enough in the great pleasures, the many pleasures, given you by God, and not to recognize them?"[15] Here he is attacking pagans for treating spectacles as outlets of pleasure, forgetting the greater pleasures one may obtain from faith. "What greater pleasure is there ...[here is a long list of new pleasures appropriate for a believer]...These are the pleasures, the spectacles of Christians, holy, eternal, and free. Here find your games of the circus..."[16] What this passage and the following analogies reveal is that there will always be a pathos of spectacle, new spectacles will replace the old ones, this is now how we will consider what spectacle is. The cult value of spectacular experiences has fallen into oblivion since the Romans. The medieval age was not interested in investing in artistic spectacles in their manifold since God's spectacle was sufficient for its spirit, but it too had a certain pathos of spectacle. The early moderns, the Renaissance, tried to pick up the pieces and the fragments to re-work it into great public spectacles.

§ 87

The relationship between myth and spectacle is strong and intimate in ancient Greek culture.[6] The historical and spiritual connection between theater and the cult of Dionysus notwithstanding, the Greek theater presented myths on stage, by revitalizing them in performance. The question as to how to present gods on stage did not arise in early theater, because they were already godly and mythic (this question arises later with Euripides in whose times myths come under the scrutiny of rational ex-

---

6   I was struck by the parallels, at the symbolic level, between the Greek tragedy and the Japanese Noh drama during my visit to Japan in 1994. No doubt, there are many divergences between the two owing to their different historical and socio-cultural contexts. However, they are both mythic theaters that use elements of dance, music, acting, masks and other visual devices. The Greek theater is closely linked to Greek mythology and the cult of Dionysus whereas the Noh theater is embedded in Shintoism and its animistic spirits. In terms of subject-matter, Greek tragedy would be closer to Waki Noh and Shura Mono genres which have, respectively, gods/demigods and heroes/warriors as their themes. Although I do not know Japanese, the symbolism of the Noh theater had a deep impression on my soul (I could not understand why half of the audience was asleep during the performance I had attended).

amination). The separation between spectacle and myth starts when human beings let their own mythic part (or self) fall into oblivion; at this point they no longer see themselves as godly and heroic.

§ 88

Nietzsche claims in *The Birth of Tragedy*[17] that the various masks used on the stage were the masks of Dionysus and the stories told reflected Dionysian wisdom. I agree with this finding to some extent, that is, to the extent that tragic stage presents the wisdom of ecstasy in one way or another (the wisdom that says all perish and all are one). But I do not agree with it if Nietzsche is saying that tragic stage re-presents only one type of cult-wisdom, namely, that of Dionysus (this would go against Nietzsche's own *agonal* way of thinking). On the contrary, tragedies bring to presence a variety of cult-wisdoms from different cults that have to do with death, sacrifice, vengeance (against matricide), friendship unto death, power-broking, family law and honor, and so on. Some of these do not even have close connection with the cult of Dionysus.

§ 89

In ancient myths where epic stories about heroes were kept alive in folk traditions (in music, dance, and song) and in their elevation to and expression in different artistic media by poets, both the "popular" and the "classic" were sustained together in a unity in their hierarchical relation according to the poets. Such dichotomies as the popular vs. the classic (or the low vs. the high) do not exist in them. The folk needs to express itself in its art forms, the poet needs to elevate them to higher artistic forms in that art medium.

§ 90

In the modern age, the myth becomes convoluted and confounded with nationhood; this is mostly due to the rise of the nation-state concept and nationalisms in our age and its emphasis on the strictly political (Wagner, for instance, does not think through this philosophical problem). And in this way the modern experience of myths betrays, to some extent, the very universality that myths aspire to.[7]

---

7   One major problem in modernity is that political/military leaders become the highest icons (they present themselves as such and/or are treated by their followers as such). What is clearly a blasphemy in the mythic age now becomes the norm which is a socio-pathology of egoism (a special brand of ego-making). If there were gods above these heroes, there would then perhaps be a limit to this type of egoism. But now cities are adorned with the monumental sculptures of these leaders; urban dwellers are constantly reminded of their unbroken hegemony. However, the masses do not realize that following greatness in this way (if the leaders are indeed great) does not make them like the great leaders but more unlike them. Art, on the other hand, can deal with such human icons differently: in the works of Cem Aydoğan, modern day icons are shown in different sizes, they are made not of bronze or marble, but in dough, bread, or chocolate. They are human, all too human.

Chapter 5: Feeling, Violence, and Catharsis

§ 91

Artistic spectacles bring out a variety of human emotions ranging on the rich spectrum from joy to suffering or any other axis of emotions. Some of these emotions are ineffable; there are simply no words to express them. The depth and the expanse of human emotions is no excuse for castigating them, as some philosophers have demanded.

§ 92

The modern human being is incapable of suffering profoundly; all is empty, all is on the surface. This incapacity shows itself in the entertainment industry. To view art and to experience spectacle solely for entertainment must be unique to our age. What does entertainment really mean? That it is all about joy and pleasure? But can joy and pleasure be separated from suffering and pain? This initially Socratic problem, which has passed through many phases, has now come down to its most shallow, utilitarian phase: avoid pain at all costs, art is to be all about entertainment.

§ 93

Socrates said that the feelings of pain and pleasure do not exist at the same time in the same person (see *Phaedo*). Based on this ontological separation, the Stoics denied pleasure and embraced pain whereas the Epicureans accepted pleasure (primarily passive pleasure) and promoted the avoidance of pain. Christian saints, following on the Stoic tradition, tortured themselves to be ecstatic and to simulate the sufferings of Christ. Utilitarians, on the other hand, following the Epicurean tradition, called for avoidance of all pain and for maximizing pleasure and happiness. The contemporary pathos of pain and pleasure and the entertainment industry that relies on it are taking this ontological dualism as given.

§ 94
Both pain and pleasure belong to the economy of human existence, and any feeling that has to do with pain or pleasure (or any other feeling) is a part of the *economy* of spectacle.

§ 95
Suffering brings depth and intensity, joy lightness and playfulness to spectacular relations.

§ 96
According to Aristotle, tragedy accomplishes the catharsis of the emotions of "pity and terror." The tragic spectator suffers with the characters on stage and is terrified at their fall (at their usually violent end). The spectator is saddened and cries during such scenes. On the other hand, comedy achieves the catharsis of the pleasure of laughter. Whether the spectator cries in a tragedy or laughs in a comedy, these discharges (that the spectators may not experience elsewhere) are necessary for human life. In agreement with Aristotle, we can add that there is a spectrum of emotions that artistic spectacles evoke in spectators, which can strengthen their emotional make-up. The problem here is not that spectacles evoke emotions in spectators (contra Plato), but rather what kinds of emotions they evoke. Do they elevate the

spectators with noble sentiments or debase them with lowly sentiments? Do the emotional elements of spectacle overwhelm the spectators, leaving them no space to feel their own individual emotional responses?

§ 97

A variety of feelings flows into the making of an artwork and its spectacle.[8] Although it may be at times difficult to detect what these feelings are, they are usually there and make their impact on the spectators (this is more so with artistic spectacles that have dramatic components). Furthermore, when we examine the spectrum of human feelings, we see that some feelings come from the higher self, some from the lower self and, under optimum circumstances, it is desirable to know what is high and what is low and to retain them as such both in the lives of individuals and in the life of a culture. Now this is not to say that certain low feelings should not be presented in artistic spectacles; on the contrary, it is necessary to show them, albeit in their proper place and relation to higher feelings (Nietzsche's critique of Wagner's romanticism and promotion of weak sentimental feelings can be understood in this context). In agreement with some of the sages of the past, I consider the following human feelings as stemming from the lower self and propose that they be treated as such by artists and spectacle-makers: pity, revenge, *ressentiment*, punishment, jealousy, and altruism.

---

8   In *Johnny Guitar*, for instance, I see the major conflict in the domain of feelings as the conflict between love (and its related feelings) and vengefulness.

§ 98
Catharsis and its role, however, must be understood in their spectacular context. In other words, catharsis is not the goal or the function of arts and artistic spectacles as Aristotle may have conceived it to be, since arts serve no utilitarian function or purpose. If, on the other hand, artistic spectacles are used for some purpose (as in art therapy, for instance, for the purpose of healing), this needs to be placed within its own context. Artistic spectacles can be therapeutic indirectly and cannot be defined only in terms of this function.

§ 99
Catharsis, in earlier times, had cult value and was practiced for the purposes of religious purification; the cult member had to be "purified" in order to approach the deity in any of his/her forms. Purification was carried out with water, fire, smoke, or air. There are some opposing tendencies between the religious exercise of catharsis and its later spectacular function: in the former, the believer goes through catharsis before the experience of religious spectacle; in the latter, however, the spectator experiences catharsis during the spectacle itself.

§ 100
One other possible problem in catharsis that Nietzsche observes is the burdening of the spectator with sentiments (this happens when the emotional part of the spectacle exceeds its limits and tries to efface other 'effects'). Nietzsche says: "Just look at the Greek tragic poets to see what it was that most excited their industry, their inventiveness, their competition: certainly not the attempt to overwhelm the spectator with senti-

ments."¹⁸ Here the target of the polemic can be both Aristotle and the romantics. Such sentimentalism, according to Nietzsche, would weaken the spectator by not allowing much room for individual experience of the spectacle.

§ 101
With a calling for a mythic, magical theater without reverting back to the old myths, Artaud attempted to create an integral experience of spectacle that would engulf both the heart and the senses, that is, the whole being of the spectator. The theater of cruelty would shake the spectators with violent scenes, scenes of crime, love, war, and madness. "Everything that acts is a cruelty. It is upon this idea of extreme action, pushed beyond all limits, that theater must be built."¹⁹ Intensification of action, shocking the spectator, appealing to the whole being (the idea of total spectacle) and gathering around new interpretations of myths: these, among others, are the ways, for Artaud, to create a new spectacular experience.⁹

§ 102
Violence is necessary to attack the spectator and shake all the organs. To say that violence in the spectacle would lead to the exacerbation of social problems, as argued by moralists today

---

9 The play *Requiem Aeternam Deo*, directed by Fulya Peker that I saw in April 2007 in New York, had many such Artaudian elements of violence, crime, love, and madness (within a mythically bound context): the play opens with Nietzsche's madman announcing the death of God; one of the tightrope walkers drops dead and is buried by Zarathustra; Zarathustra is bitten by the adder; and Zarathustra expresses love for the overhuman, that is, he *loves* in a human that which is always overcoming itself. I am thankful to Peker, Rainer J. Hanshe, and the actors for bringing such a difficult and an untimely figure on stage.

and in the past, would be as ridiculous as to claim that nudity in spectacle would cause orgasmic responses from the spectators. The portrayal of violent scenes that are detached from their mythic/sacred base may contribute to social violence among the spectators for whom violence and the experience of the sacred are already disenfranchised.

§ 103

I claim, on the contrary, that scenes of death, violence and sacrifice contribute to the creation of ecstatic states and communion among the spectators and a strong bond between the spectators and the spectacle (with the expectation of overcoming the ontological separation between the S and the s). One may wonder why human beings have always been drawn to spectacles of torture and suffering. Foucault gives the example of Damiens' execution in France, and Bataille says he was haunted all throughout his life by the image of the torture of the Chinese regicide. Perhaps these examples do not belong to the domain of artistic spectacles *per se*, but they do highlight the human fascination with violence and violent scenes. It is not only that human beings derive pleasure from the sufferings of others—this too is an undeniable human tendency for which there exists a word in German, *Schadenfreude*, but also in the spectacle of suffering one sees too one's own suffering and mortality (the ability to do this is an ecstatic function). When ancient Greek spectators watched Prometheus in chains on stage, it is highly unlikely that they derived pleasure from his sufferings. The power factor also plays a role here: it is a matter of looking up to higher types (as in the case of gods and heroes in tragedy) and a matter of looking

84

down at lower types (as is the case with comedies, according to Aristotle).

§ 104
If Bataille is right in his observation that taboos on death and sexuality are the strongest taboos in human societies, then the presentation of transgression of these taboos would bring a certain dimension and depth to spectacle and most likely cause a certain profound imprint on the spectator. Scenes of murder, sacrifice, incestuous affairs, erotic acts, orgies would be such elements of transgression, and Greek tragedies used most of these elements to create such depth and imprint on the audience without necessarily presenting them directly on stage. How these elements are used and presented by the artists is as important as how they are received by the spectators; this brings us to the issue of context. Let us repeat: not every spectacle is for every one.

§ 105
For instance, presentation of sex scenes (or "objects of desire") is not a problem in itself, but again the question is that of context. The dominant type of presentation of sex in today's age is *pornographic* (that has become possible in the age of mass production) and is pervasive throughout society (the pornographic is not to be found only in what is called pornography). Or, let us put it in another way: mechanization of sexual acts, stripping sex (and the body in general) of its sacred worth, treating human beings as mere instruments (for commercial purposes for the most part), negative/reactive forms of power, superficiality, absence of imagination, all of these gained currency due to mass reproduction. The pornographic culture[20] can be combated only by an

erotic culture where sexuality is restored to its sacred context and presented thus in spectacle (an open sea to embark upon for the eroticists).

§ 106
Eroticism in the domain of sexuality is analogous to the total artwork in the domain of arts. It activates and brings together all human functions in the sexual life of a human being; in the erotic act, one becomes fractured but yet whole again. Therefore, erotic spectacles are needed to cultivate an erotic culture;[21] however, such spectacles must be bound within a mythic context and, as a result, have cult value. Or else, artistic spirits among whom erotic urges flow upwards, will shy away from bringing their erotic works into spectacle. We can assume that the satyr plays in Greek theater had such a function; they have gradually decayed into vulgar, banal sex shows (analogous to today's empty sex shows), especially in the Roman theater (this was what the Early Church Fathers reacted to in the last centuries of the Roman Empire).

§ 107
Spectacles of violence, death, and sex cannot be shown to anyone at any time, because they are bound within a sacred context and demand their own *cult*ivated spectators who can experience them in a profound and meaningful way (meaningful to them and to their relations with others). Here what is at stake is not only the stage of life that one is in, but the necessary level of cultivation and initiation that one has. The mass society has obliterated all such concerns and boundaries.

Chapter 6: The Unconscious and Transference in Body and the Soul

§ 108

Unconscious forces are always at work and are everywhere. In artistic spectacles, however, what the public is faced with is a moment in the cloud of the unconscious of the artist made available in a specific medium with the help of the makers of spectacle.

§ 109

The unconscious is, in Freud, the domain of the id in his second topography of the psyche in which he splits it into three parts: the id, the ego, and the superego. For a well-balanced psyche (if such a thing could exist in this age), all parts must fulfill their functions and act in some coordination with one another. The unconscious forces (creative and destructive energies of Eros and Thanatos) must sublimate themselves in a particular way and into a particular outlet; the ego sustains the reality principle (connection with the outside world); and the superego functions as the moral agent, the agent of coordination in some sense. If we apply this topography to artistic spectacles, we realize that the psychic relations are constantly displaced and restructured through their impact primarily on the id (via the ego and the superego where the ego is the conduit for the impact and the superego the control switch). Ultimately (and under optimum circumstances) artistic spectacles can help create "healthy" psyches and psychic balances.

§ 110

The unconscious, though popularized by Freud, cannot be confined to its psychoanalytic meaning. On the contrary, it is necessary to keep in mind its cosmic and cultural significance. That the unconscious is prior to the conscious simply signifies that a) one's individual awareness or collective awareness and all that is based on this such as knowledge is limited (i.e. one cannot know everything), b) there are many actual and possible interpretations of existence (i.e. perspectivism) and one cannot be the sum-total of such interpretations, and c) consciousness is only a thin slice on the surface of the ocean of unconsciousness.

§ 111

An individual's unconscious is not necessarily locked away from his or her gaze entirely; it depends on one's disposition and one's courage, profundity, readiness to face one's own death, and honesty so that one can be at the gateway of the unconscious peeking inside. Kofman's analogy of *camera obscura* explains the relationship between the vast depository of the unconscious and what comes out through the gateway. There are many negatives waiting for the creator, but one must be able to fetch them and have the means, the tools, and the medium to channel them into an artwork and this artwork into a public spectacle. This type of access to the unconscious is vital to artistic creation, though not sufficient by itself.

§ 112

There is a connection, which usually remains hidden from most, between the unconscious of the artist and the unconscious of the spectators in a given artistic spectacle. In other words, a spectacle is a contact point between the former and the latter; therefore, much that is transmitted in a spectacular experience remains unconscious (this is why, more often than not, we cannot express with words why and how some parts of a particular spectacle have affected us). This artistic transmission too is a manifestation of the unconscious analogous to Freud's dreams, jokes, and slips of the tongue.

§ 113
The unconscious must be understood not only in the psychic sense (as in dreams), but also in the somatic sense as the life of instincts and drives. Artistic spectacles, therefore, reactivate both the psychic and the somatic forces in the lives of the spectators.

§ 114
The human body is vibrant, vital, and a growing being that consists of many senses, organs, functions, liquids, and so on. All of these must be activated and moved[10] in spectacular experi-

---

10 In our age performance artists try to achieve this by using different types of media during the same performance. One such performance artist whose work I recently experienced is Jaime del Val. In his metaformance there are several plains of immanence, which crisscross one another in ways that exceed ordinary understanding; these plains are body-body parts, sound, and digital projection. The performer, who appears, with all the gadgets attached to his body, as though he just landed on earth from another planet—in his outdoor performances he looks like a naked astronaut—walks around in and out of his audience in slow motions, as he coordinates his movements and projections with what is projected on the screen. Body parts, removed from their home, are now amplified, deformed, and transfigured. They are no longer recognizable as body parts on the screen; they create a different landscape and as such are transfigurations in a digital medium.

ences. All of them *belong together* in one body; why would a spectacle affect our eyes and ears and leave all the other senses and organs unaffected? Scriabin, for instance, blended colors and smells with his music and took a step towards synaesthesia.

§ 115
Synaesthesia (from Greek, joint perception) is a sensation in one part of the body produced by a stimulus applied to another part. Shrill sounds, for instance, can produce sensations in the flesh. A sound can invoke an image (called *photism*) or, vice versa, an image can cause the spectator to hear a sound (called *phonism*). Synaesthesia, which has a neurological dimension, has also to do with imagination (conscious or unconscious) and is central to the idea of total artwork.

§ 116
Myths bring together the psychic and somatic unconscious forces and give them a temporal unity and direction.

§ 117
Every act of creation is a carrying over, that is, an *übertragung*, a transference. Images, sounds, symbols, feelings, states of the body, blocks of sense-perception are carried over from one place to another in the combusting and bursting spirit of the artist. Nietzsche uses the term within a linguistic context as he explains the process of the creation of words. In Freud, on the other hand, the term is used within a psychic context as he explains how the dreams function. I propose to use this term for spectacular experiences.

§ 118
At one point what is carried over is given a semblance of unity, what is called an art work, and this then is carried over to the public domain. The locus of the artistic spectacle seems like a stagnant place to many (especially to the somnambulistic moderns), but this locus is a point of passage of a torrential stream. In this regard, moderns look like cows that are entering into a roaring river without feeling its violence.

§ 119
To be in tune with this stream of transference, spectators must also be in motion, flying around the spectacle. This will enable them to be open to a variety of stimuli and to experience the spectacle from different perspectival points in three-dimensions.

§ 120
The Surrealists, a name for a diversity of artists, writers, and thinkers, *agreed* on the primacy of the unconscious forces. Breton promoted the idea of spontaneous writing that would allow the writer to plunge freely into his/her unconscious. Dali's paintings where images are disfigured, shuffled, contracted, and expanded are close to dream-like states. Bataille, a stranger to surrealism, expressed ecstatic states in bizarre scenes in his erotic writings. And finally, Artaud, an oddball in the movement, developed a form of theater that is mythic and visceral. These examples and others from the works of the so-called surrealists underlie the importance of the unconscious in the making of arts and experiencing artworks in artistic spectacles.

Chapter 7: Movement

§ 121

Movement has always existed. And neither language nor the intellect is sufficiently equipped to understand concrete movement, as Bergson showed in his *Matter and Memory*. This is analogous to human feelings that language cannot adequately express, but even more complicated than that, because feelings are human feelings, whereas movement belongs to all types of beings. And there are probably more types of movements than types of human feelings.

§ 122

Most of the inner forces of spectacle already connote movement: in ecstasy there is a motion from one state to another, imagination is a shuffling of images or a free play among faculties of the mind, and unconscious transference is a type of movement.

§ 123

All things are in motion, all things are becoming. Therefore, movement has to do with change and becoming. Being is only a semblance of permanence, which, for a culture, may be a necessary illusion (that sense of permanence is much older than our recent metaphysics of Being) and can perhaps be traced back to the archaic layer of the psyche of the first settled human beings. If Being weighs heavily upon us, we would not be able to move our bodies and dance. This type of heavy Being lies in recent history and plays as a counter-force to living up to re-creating life as movement.

§ 124
There is movement in our inner lives, more, faster, and deeper in some than others. However, in the midst of everyday activities, this inner movement can easily be forgotten. What the eye cannot see (and if one follows the dictates of the eye), it dismisses as invalid. Such inner movements and other movements that are undetectable by the naked eye are often relegated to the status of non-existence.

§ 125
Modern dance is appealing not only on account of the magic and the aesthetic of body/movement (both of these exist in ballet and other body arts). What is more striking about it is how an everyday body/movement can be remolded and elevated to a different height and the fact that its repertoire is attuned to the variety of the states of the body. In this sense it approximates the dances of the gods (what is called *theopraxis*).[22]

§ 126
Modern dance breaks down the body/movement into its minutest components and reconstructs them anew.

§ 127
Modern dance brings the human body back in touch and in tune with *physis*.

§ 128

In addition to the invention of the devices of moving images, what is unique to our age are the devices that can channel the movement of electrons. At the foundation of all electric, electronic, and digital technology lies this movement. Now the movement of electrons exists in nature, but in this age we are capable of channeling these movements into new areas as our ancestors could channel water, air, fire or metal in the different phases of their history. Spectacle-makers who rely significantly on the use of this recent technology (such as the digital artists) *must* understand this basic fact and confront *electronic* movement in its rudimentary form. Electrons, just like the human body or images, move in different ways (smoothly, slowly or fast, jumping in an avalanche as in semi-conductors, etc.) What is uncanny about their movement, however, is that they evade basic human perception.

§ 129

Whether it is the movement of a dancer, an image, a sound, an atom, or an electron, at bottom we are faced with a phenomenology of movement, which, in its essence, is unpredictable, spontaneous, and fragmentary; it is us, in our desire to be secure, who make movement predictable, non-spontaneous, and unitarian. Movement is explosive and implosive at the same time.

Chapter 8: Language, Text, Music, and Image

§ 130

In accordance with our western logocentric heritage, we have been accustomed to focus on the linguistic aspect of artistic spectacles: we want to understand before we experience a spectacle. Its end-result is a partial experience of the spectacle. This trend is still strong in today's society, but has been attacked by thinkers and artists alike going as far back as Schopenhauer along two axes: language/music and language/image.

§ 131

Schopenhauer claims, in his major work *World as Will and Representation*,[23] that music is the most universal art form and is more universal than language (or concepts) since it is a direct objectification of the will and belongs not to the phenomenal world (the world of forms and ideas), but to the *noumenal* world: "...it is clear that music expresses in an exceedingly universal language, in a homogeneous material, that is, in mere tones, and with the greatest distinctness and truth, the inner being, the in-itself, of the world, which we think of under the concept of will, according to its most distinct manifestation."[24] Although Schopenhauer attempts to retrieve music from the clutches of the intellect and abstract language, he goes to another extreme when he elevates music above all arts.

§ 132

Schopenhauer's thesis that music is not formal or phenomenal must be examined. Does he mean that music is neither tangible nor visible? This should not be difficult to understand, and, consequently, one cannot relate to music with the categories of the visible. But if he means that there is no ordering (no logos as gathering) in music, he would be wrong, although the musical ordering is different from, let's say, linguistic ordering. Let it suffice here to say that musical experience is different and must not be subordinated to the limited ability of the intellect and abstract language.

§ 133
Wagner followed Schopenhauer on the priority of music over all arts and language and composed his *Tristan und Isolde* under the influence of his philosophy. Music has to create the mood first and evoke appropriate emotions; visual presentations and the drama follow later. Wagner took this ordering into account in his vision for the architecture of theater where the musicians are situated in the invisible abyss between the stage and the audience.

§ 134
In agreement with Schopenhauer and Wagner, Nietzsche claims that language cannot express adequately either reality in general or music. "Language can never adequately render the cosmic symbolism of music..." (BT, p.55) Here language is associated with the phenomenal world. "...hence *language*, as the organ and symbol of phenomena, can never by any means disclose the innermost heart of music..."[25]

§ 135
Another problem in the Schopenhauerean line of thought is to make one part of human existence superior over to other parts: the musical over the visual and the plastic. This may be

pleasing to the ego of a Schopenhauerean composer, but is of no use for culture-making or for spectacular experiences. The Schopenhauerean rebellion against western rationalism and its metaphysics of the visible can be accepted to some extent, but not in its extreme form. Schopenhauer himself does not think of the problem of time when he separates the visible from the audible in such a metaphysical way.

§ 136
On the other hand, language and image relationship has not been without its problems in our spectacular experiences. According to Foucault, the playful, chiasmic relation between text and image has been disrupted by classical representation (in painting) in two ways: "the first asserts the separation between plastic representation (which implies resemblance) and linguistic reference (which excludes it)."[26] Here one or the other rules, but in either case, there is no agonistic sustenance of both as in their chiasmic relation (as it exists in a calligram). "The second principle...posits an equivalence between the fact of resemblance and the affirmation of a representative bond." Here a statement imposes itself, implicitly or explicitly, on the work of art; it says "what you see is that."[27] The former problem is addressed by Klee and the latter by Kandinsky. And Magritte, the main subject of Foucault's *This is not a pipe*, is operating within the space of transformation of these two principles of classical representation.

§ 137
We can draw the following conclusions from Foucault's reflections on language within the context of painting and its spectacle: artistic spectacles do not represent some reality by dictating

what it is linguistically; a signifier or a statement need not determine an individual's experience of a particular spectacle or the spectacle itself; in artistic spectacles all those forces that are human, including texts and images, may enter into a playful game that is and can be experienced on the part of the spectator. No one force should lord over others in a hegemonic way.

§ 138
No doubt we human beings are linguistic beings, and we like to talk. If we were only linguistic beings, there would not be any spectacle; we would be just chatting. We are linguistic beings, but we are so many other things at the same time. A piece of wise saying may help here: "there is time to talk and time to remain silent." We are accustomed to reduce an experience to its linguistic aspect, either before or after the experience. However, the experience remains irreducible; it resists such a reduction more in some people than in others.

§ 139
On the other hand, poetic ambiguity is the landmark of artistic spectacles. It makes the linguistic text (if it exists in the spectacle) richer and opens itself up to a variety of readings by individual spectators. Sophocles is considered to be a master of ambiguity;[28] in his text the same word can be understood in different ways by the two characters who use it in the same dialogue. As a result, tragedy flows back and forth in the tension between transparency and ambiguity on the spectrum from the poet to the spectator via the theatrical medium: "It is only for the spectator that the language of the text can be transparent at every level in all its polyvalence and with all its ambiguities. Be-

tween the author and the spectator the language thus recuperates the full function of communication that it has lost on the stage between the protagonists in the drama. But the tragic message, when understood, is precisely that there are zones of opacity and incommunicability in the words that men exchange."[29]

§ 140

Another example for poetic ambiguity is from the poetry of the troubadours who used coded language in their performances. It had to be deciphered by their spectators in different ways depending on their social status and position in the circle of fine love (*fin amor*). This style of coded language, called *trobar clus*, was perfected by such poets as Marcabru and Cardenal. The ambiguity in artistic spectacles has a correlation to the hierarchy of spectators which can be illustrated in a diagram:

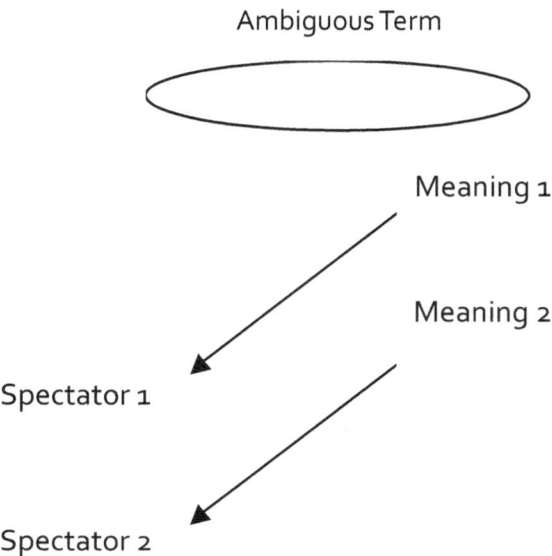

In the tragic spectacle, ambiguity is reverberated both within the stage (among the characters), between the stage and the audience, and within the audience. Since the troubadours engaged in mostly small performances, there could have been no such reverberations on the stage on a grand scale as it had existed on the Greek stage.

Chapter 9: Thinking and the Intellect

§ 141
There is a certain type of thinking that works with abstractions, categorizes with unchanging concepts, classifies, and orders; it is called abstract thinking and is detached from insights and feelings. It is also referred to as the intellect. It unifies by way of homogeneity (reduction to the same), it tends to expand into other territories (like a naughty boy who does not know his limits), and considers itself eternal. In addition, it is reflective and discursive (it expands over time and it builds immediately on previous constructs).

§ 142
The other kind of thinking relies on intuitions and insights; let us call this 'intuitive thinking.' This type of thinking just happens momentarily and is in close contact with feelings, dreams, and instincts. Arts and artistic spectacles function more with intuitive thinking than abstract thinking; abstract thought, in fact, hinders the artistic process.

§ 143
Abstract thinking claims that everything must be known and must be submitted to the higher court of consciousness and the intellect. Once this becomes universally accepted in a culture, all other forces and functions diminish in value.

§ 144
A culture that promotes only abstract thinking emaciates, consciously or unconsciously (mostly the latter), its poetic, mythic, and ecstatic functions. In addition to the intellectualization of

culture, what one witnesses are its politicization, moralization and gradual popularization, an occurrence that the founders of the intellectual culture would not have predicted.

§ 145
The fact that sciences have their own spectacles will relieve artistic spectacles from the burden of intellectualization of the artistic process and artistic spectacles.

§ 146
The invention of the photographic camera has created a new type of a fusion between the arts and the sciences.

§ 147
On the other hand, sciences can enter into a playful relation with arts and allow their basic building blocks to be re-created in different artistic media; just as concepts and words can be played with in poetry and thus re-created, they can also be re-created in other artistic media. Conceptual art is possible in that cultural space where sciences no longer interfere with the artistic domain and art is no longer understood rigidly and narrowly as the production of works of art.

§ 148
Every work of art, every artistic spectacle, however chaotic it may seem, has a 'concept' behind it. Instead of the term 'concept,' I prefer to use the term 'logos' since the former has the connotation of being static and stagnant. This logos, in conjunction with the myth of that spectacle, is the underlying principle according to which all the pieces that make the work and its spectacle possible are gathered together and about which one can speak.

§ 149

Artistic spectacles are imbibed with a certain philosophical mood that is the imprint of their creators and their world-views, and this mood becomes manifest in spectacle in different degrees depending on the dispositions of the individual spectators. Optimism, pessimism, idealism, realism, materialism, romanticism, and sentimentalism are some such moods. If the mood is already problematic from a philosophical standpoint, then the spectators are burdened with a mood that would creep into their being in a surreptitious way.

§ 150

Philosophical wisdom can be present in artistic spectacles implicitly, subtly, playfully and without intruding into their mythopoeic functions and be re-presented in innovative ways; and more importantly the performative nature of philosophy[11] can be brought out. The poetic wisdom one finds in Aeschylus's plays and their spectacles, for instance, is far more interesting, more colored, more imaginative and thought-provoking than Aristotle's ethical platitudes.

---

11 Since Kierkegaard and Nietzsche there has been a trend towards theatrical philosophy; Martin Puchner calls this a 'theatrical turn' in philosophy. This is not the case only with philosophers who have engaged with theater and dramatic literature directly (as with Sartre and Camus, for instance), but also with thinkers who, like the Cynics, consider philosophical action as performance such as Deleuze. There are many performance artists, thinkers, and scholars who are currently working on this fusion between philosophy and performance. One such group, called "Generating Bodies: Philosophy on Stage," is based in Vienna and is headed by Arno Böhler. I was fortunate to have seen his and Susanne Granzer's performance at the Deutsches Haus in New York. Their project is concerned with exposing the performative aspect of knowledge by using different artistic elements on stage.

Chapter 10: Science and Technology

§ 151

A certain body of knowledge and a certain type of *techne* go into the making of any spectacle within the historical context of the making of that particular spectacle. The ancient Greeks invested a great deal of their scientific knowledge and technological skill into theater building. Even a simple spectacle would take certain skills and the use of tools to create. But, in no age other than ours that is knowable to the historians, what is produced in and by technology took the upper hand and shaped the very core of human existence, including our spectacular relations.

§ 152

It is Heidegger's claim that technology is not only the know-what and know-how of certain tools, but in the age of technology it becomes the essence of our being-in-the-world. The technological *Dasein* sees all beings as numbers and treats them as standing reserve, ready to be put into use in the mechanical, industrial complex and everyday work. Nature and human beings are simply things or instruments to be used; nothing is any longer singularly precious or sacred. The age of the masses is the age of instrumentalization.

§ 153

That our *Dasein* has become technological simply means that we have come to live, experience everything in a technological way, which includes our spectacular experiences and relations. Now anyone who learns how to use a tool and pick up a camera claims to be an artist; for the ancient Greeks to be a poet was something sacred, precious, reserved for the few, the one who was inspired or *enthusiastic*. But, according to Heidegger, this mode of being-in-the-world is revelatory; technological *Dasein* reveals its mode of being. And only through this revelation and its recognition, it can be overcome. Therefore, technology must be confronted in itself. Great artistic spirits to whom technological *Dasein* reveals itself in art will confront technology and will bring this confrontation to the public sphere in spectacles.

§ 154
Benjamin's notion of the work of art in the age of technological reproduction represents a radical shift in the pathos of spectacle in our recent past and must be understood within the context of an epochal shift. Other such shifts in the history of Occidental civilization includes the rise of Greek theater (the beginning of the S/s cut), the spectacle of Christ on the Cross (see Tertullian) for the medievals, and the revival of classical Greco-Roman arts for the early moderns. The recent post-classical shift in the pathos of spectacle also includes, among other things, the rise of Impressionism in painting, the re-introduction of the total artwork, and the transformation of classical theater into mythico-magical theater.

§ 155
Bringing Heidegger and Benjamin together, one can say that they are in agreement on the alienating aspect of technology. For Heidegger it is the mode of technological being-in-the-world that alienates us from Being; for Benjamin the technological reproduction destroyed the traditional fabric of the works of art—

hence the de-contextualization in our age—and the uniqueness of works of art (due to mass appeal), both of which contribute to alienation. The move towards authenticity would entail a gathering of *techne* in a poetic fashion that turns towards Being and its truth and a gathering together of the fragments of the shattered aura in new contexts and in new art forms.

§ 156
The challenge for the new artists is then to cultivate a new cult value for new art forms and spectacles (this will counteract the exchange value that the bourgeois order dictates). Installation art, for instance, does this by making itself unmarketable (a resistance from within).

§ 157
Another challenge is to experience and show the integrity of the creative act, of poesy (to close the open wound of modern *techne*). Whether it is making tools or artifacts or works of art, all creations belong to that act of making. If this were to be accepted, if most human beings looked at their creative deeds as integral, as sacred, as bound to their own selves, as their unique and authentic expressions, there would be less rubbish in the world today. Again the total artwork and, in recent times, installation art that uses live performance strive to present human life as integral.

Chapter 11: Space and Place

§ 158
We have a certain inner condition (or predisposition), what Kant calls inner form of intuition, that is *a priori* and that enables us to experience places, locations, distances, etc. and gives us a sense of where we are vis-à-vis other objects, persons in nature and in the universe. That condition is space, and all the others shall be called 'place'; therefore, place is grounded in space. Although Kant located space strictly in the human mind, we will re-locate it in the entire human existence. Moreover, space/place relations vary from epoch to epoch.

§ 159
In every experience of spectacle, we are both in space and in a place. Every spectacle happens in a place that is shaped by the conditions of space. Most Greek theaters were built on the slope of hills, but, at the same time, followed a mathematical and symmetric precision that created a perfect acoustics outdoors. Human calculation and construction in a natural setting; a harmonious fusion between culture and nature. All of these must have happened with a certain notion of space.

§ 160
Spectacular relations are constituted, among other things, by the spatial constructs of their historical era. Distances, places, how to arrange the spectacle to be presented (including the works of art) and the spectacular positions are all functions of these spatial constructs. The artist has and works with a notion of space that is projected onto the cultural domain in spectacle. Re-

naissance artists introduced perspectivism in painting, which was becoming a space construct in that time period; in other words, their version of perspectivism (perspectival drawing) corresponded to the thought of perspectivism that was prevalent at that time. Therefore, perspectivism in spectacle complemented the thought of perspectivism in culture, among the spectators of Renaissance art.

§ 161
Perspectivism, however, cannot be confined to the visual technique as conceived by the Renaissance artist who invented it in order to represent depth and distance in the visual medium. From a broader and spectacular standpoint, each spectacle and all the spectators are situated perspectivally, in terms of all the inner forces they activate and all the spectacular *values* they uphold, both within their own internal dynamics and vis-à-vis the culture to which they belong. Spectacular perspective cannot be understood solely as a function of visual effects or physical distance, although these are included in it. Therefore, my use of perspectivism in spectacle is closer to the way it was understood by ancient Greek skeptics and by Nietzsche than to its Renaissance conception.

§ 162
Perspectivism in spectacle ultimately underlies the fact that all spectators experience a particular spectacle from their individually determined perspectival condition.

§ 163
The *Gestalt* of spectacle reflects the pathos of spectacle of the times, both of the spectacle makers and the spectators. Ancient

Greeks had outdoor Ω-shaped theaters with the orchestra at the bottom and in the middle, with the seats split into sections; their concept of space, unlike ours, was in tune with nature and natural settings, it blended with and enveloped the slope (one can see this in Wright's architectural style and also in Buddhist art). Most re-formers of spectacle think through the question of space in spectacle: Wagner, Artaud *et al*.

§ 164

Architectural spectacle as an artistic spectacle suffers, in general, from an immediate association of architecture with usefulness. This utilitarian perception of buildings and their permanence in everyday life, no doubt, takes away from experiencing them spectacularly. First, not every building is worthy of spectacular attention. Second, those that have spectacular worth shall be kept away from the general public use so as to retain their cult value.

§ 165

When a culture sinks into utilitarianism and when buildings are built entirely for immediate use value with no taste, the architectural spectacle sinks faster than any other type of artistic spectacle. Let there be architectural works to be experienced only as spectacles...

§ 166

Since ancient cities/ruins are usually not permitted to be inhabited, they present to us some of the best, non-utilitarian examples of architectural spectacles. Their preservation will contribute to a cultivated taste and experience in this area.

Chapter 12: Time and Temporality

§ 167
The other inner form of intuition in Kant is time. We are always in time; we always have a sense of time whatever this sense may be. In our age, the mechanical sense of time makes itself prominent, but in antiquity also there was a sense of time. But what time is, no one knows, although certain philosophers have delved on the question.

§ 168
The sense of time that is in tune with one's self and with the cosmos is that which brings together the cycle of creation and destruction into one unity, one thought, one image, one symbol, since all come into being and perish (this unity may happen in a variety of ways). This sense of time that the ancients upheld, that one can find in the primordial *mythic time* is what Nietzsche calls the eternal return or recurrence of the same.[30] According to this, we are both living and mortal beings; the mortality is no objection to life itself, death is no burden, no curse to life.

§ 169
Art and artistic spectacles approximate time as eternal return the thought of which lies primarily in mythic thought. In a way our connection to all things, to this cosmos, is not through some 'logos' as the Stoics formulated (since 'logos' is entirely a function of beings that can speak and think) and as the medievals accepted it, but through the eternal return according to which all come into being and disappear in the cosmic cycle of creation and destruction.

§ 170

Linear time is just one mode of time or one way of experiencing time and has become the dominant form of temporality since the post-Socratic Greeks (it also corresponds to the collapse of the mythic time). Henceforth, time is understood as a spatial construct (obvious formulation of this is in Aristotle's *Physics*). Bergson called this abstract, mathematical, linear time 'duration' as opposed to 'pure time' or 'real duration' in which all the successive states melt into one another to form an indivisible process. Everyday activities operate in measured time, arts and myths in real duration. In different experiences of time a particular implementation of measured time enters into a conflicting alliance with the cyclical time. This alliance gives a sense of time to the values and institutions of that particular culture or civilization.

§ 171

Arts and myths happen in cyclical time just like what happens in dreams. Creation and destruction follow their own unpredictable, spontaneous, back and forth pattern; a three-dimensional dance of the forces of creation and destruction played out in a matrix. An artist hardly knows the end-result of his/her creation in the beginning of the process; that is why 'work-in-progress' (or work-in-retreat) has its own sacred domain.

§ 172

Augustine explains cyclical time as eternity[31] where the past, the present, and the future coincide in the eternal moment, along with the modalities of, respectively, remembering, attending, and expecting. What this means in the artistic/mythic domain is that in the creative act the creator is projecting himself, in connection with the past, onto a future via the present moment.

§ 173
Yet another meaning of the eternal return in artistic spectacles: an artwork in spectacle brings many forces of vitality (it is about life) before a living audience, but it is also a reminder of the spectator's humility (parallel to that of the artist) before all creation (it is also about mortality). The former may be obvious for the contemporary spectators, but the latter is only a hidden fact for them.

§ 174
Therefore, the way human beings experience time collectively is neither entirely linear nor entirely cyclical, but a conflicting and friendly combination of the two in different degrees. In our age and since the Socratic Greeks, linear time has taken hold of the cyclical time, hence causing a temporal hypertrophy.

§ 175
Spectacles are firework-like *cultural* events that explode and then withdraw into a silent space in the life of a culture. They reflect, in a living moment, one of the faces of their culture. A spectacle is a moment in the flow of those that are absent and present; it is a nodal point where the dead and the living come together in a this-worldly fashion.

§ 176
There have been, no doubt, resistances, prior to Kant, to the dominant conception of time as linear since the post-Socratic

Greeks: mystics, parts of Augustine, some of the medieval philosophers who conceived time as an eternal now.

§ 177
The challenge for spectacle-makers is to re-produce and re-vitalize time as mythic time.

Appendix to Parts I and II

The Unity of Spectacle

§ 178
In the first two parts of the book, the inner and the outer forces of spectacle are separated for heuristic reasons only, for these forces are inseparable as much as skin cannot be separated from its body or the syntax of a sentence from its semantics.

§ 179
It is now necessary to bring the two types of forces of spectacle together. With this, I will tentatively close the circle of spectacular immanence. The inner forces of spectacle are re-circulated, rejuvenated within the framework of the outer forces of spectacle. Therefore, we place the inner forces in the middle of the triangle:

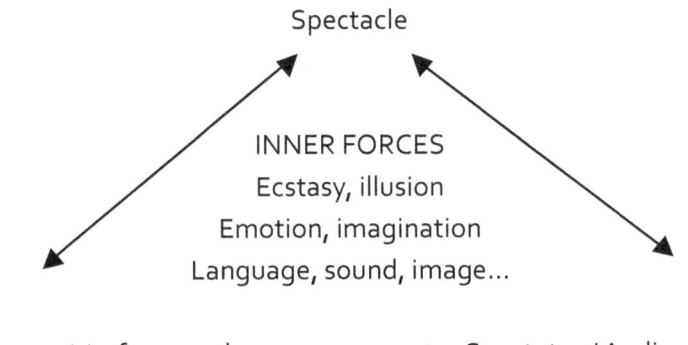

§ 180
Within the microcosm of one particular spectacle (that is situated on the larger plane of culture), the makers of spectacle operate with these forces and create an impact on their audience who are already susceptible to that impact. This impact can also be understood as power, that is, the power of spectacle. We can explain this with examples: the makers of spectacle, including the artist, recreate an artwork drawing from the collective unconscious of their culture (the macrocosm), transfer their creation onto a spectacle that connects with the unconsciousness of the spectators. The cycle does not end here especially if we bring to mind that the spectators unconsciously contribute to their culture's collective pool. We can use any of the inner forces as an example and place it in the middle of the triangle. Here we also see both the individual and the collective dimensions of spectacular experiences; one cannot be reduced to the other.

§ 181
If spectacles have *affects* on the spectators both at the level of the conscious and the unconscious, then the question one must explore here is what is it that has affects in a given spectacle? The problems in the spectacular domain will be reproduced in the unconscious of the spectator. This question of affect is closely linked to the question of power and how power and what forms of power are exercised in that specific culture. The pathos of spectacle is not isolated from other highest values (including the pathos of power) within the same epoch. Deleuze explains what affect is within the context of cinema as follows: "Affects are not individuated like people and things, but nevertheless they do not blend

into the indifference of the world. They have singularities, which enter into virtual conjunction and each time constitute a complex entity. It is like points of melting, of boiling, of condensation, of coagulation, etc."[32] Although the question of affect here is discussed within the context of movement-image and affect-image, one can speak of these and other types of affects in all spectacles (sound-affect, thought-affect, ecstasy-affect, etc). Each inner force would have its own affect or its combined affect.

§ 182

There are power relations everywhere, in every aspect of our being. The things we do may have affect on others with or without our knowledge, within or without our control. The same thing can be said for spectacular relations. Spectacles of all sorts do have varying affects on the spectators who experience them. Certain spectacles incite the audience to a rebellion, some spectacles have a numbing affect, and yet some others may have slow but deeper affect on the psyche of their spectators. One can never know the full affect of a particular spectacle on a particular spectator (for this there would have to be a barometer to measure spectacular affects), but the affect of spectacle is inevitable, and this has to do with the power that spectacle produces as it is experienced by the spectator.

§ 183

Each inner force of spectacle constitutes a directionality and becomes *power* when it hits a spectator. Therefore, spectacular power, like any other power, is not a unitary entity but is multiplistic and agonistic at its fundamental core.

§ 184
The inner forces of spectacle are not cultivated *in toto* within the spectacle, but are empowered, elevated, and given a new style there. Many other cultural formations such as mythology, literature, cults and festivals, serve as the blood supply for spectacles.

§ 185
Poetry and other literature, for instance, serve as such blood supply for spectacle. Although they are not spectacular in themselves, they anticipate spectacular relations just like a text anticipates its readers (analogous to spectacle/spectator relationship).

§ 186
We may never know fully why a particular spectator is deeply affected by a particular spectacle; not even the spectator may know this himself. This has to do with the enigmatic and multiplistic nature of power and power relations.

§ 187
Both the inner forces (semantics) and the outer forces (syntax) of spectacle exist in all forms of artistic spectacles. The same spectator may experience different types of artistic spectacles; in each case, he has entered into the triangle and some of his inner forces are re-activated in him (that is, put in motion in him). That each art form and its spectacle are unique and they therefore invoke something different in the spectator (different from other art forms) is not an objection to the thesis above. Here what is in question is not the aesthetic worth and evaluation of a work of art that must be judged according to the rules of that art form.

Granted, this may be the case, but we are in the realm of spectacle now, and spectacle has *its own language.*

§ 188
The syntax of spectacle: spectacle-makers + spectacle + spectators. All the inner forces of spectacle are present and activated within the syntax of spectacle in some form and intensity.

§ 189
Just as the outer forces of spectacle complement one another in a particular spectacle, so the inner forces point to one another even if some may remain mute or weak depending on the artistic medium (only a total artwork can activate all the inner forces). For instance, movement comes to prominence in dance and cinema; space is the medium in which architectural spectacles operate; and recent art forms of reproduction highlight technology. However, this does not mean that the other inner forces are entirely absent in the spectacles of these art forms. Certain signs that emanate from a spectacle may remain hazy, but they must not be treated as absent. Visual and plastic arts (painting and sculpture) present their subjects as motionless, but this does not mean that they do not point to movement from the standpoint of the inner forces of spectacle. Movement is latently present there.

§ 190
It is almost impossible that a spectacle, however rich and deep it may be, could activate all the inner forces of spectacle—this may though be the desire of the total artist.

§ 191
A spectacle is whole when the inner forces it activates are *organically* blended, when they are not eclectically added to one another, and when the form and the content are infused and integrated into one another. In the mythic age, one could achieve this *organic* unity through mythopoeic functions.

§ 192
With the help of the inner forces it can activate, a spectacle should be able to uplift the spectator, move him sideways, pull him towards itself, and push him back to his own perspectival position.

§ 193
Certain forms of artistic spectacles present *chiasmically* bound agonistic playfulness of the inner forces of spectacle. Calligram and calligraphy are good examples for such playfulness between image and text. And in the cinematographic medium, movement and image enter into such playful relation forming what Deleuze calls movement/image.

§ 194
The signs that a spectacle gives out point to one another as they revolve around that which is absent. The former has to do with the immanence of spectacle, that is, that spectacle does not

represent another reality, but is self-referential[12] (analogous to what Saussure says about language); the latter, on the other hand, has to do with what holds the spectacle together. I call this the 'cipher' of spectacle (it is also part of the myth that underlies each spectacle); this can be the parts of a canvas that are not painted or where there are no figures, or the silence in-between notes, or some empty area on the stage or an absent figure that is invoked. A spectacle that bombards the spectator with images and sounds and other things diminishes that space and the mythic function of the cipher (most mass-produced movies do this today).

§ 195
Although spectacles have their own immanence, their own domain and internal dynamics, they operate within a larger cultural and historical context. And as such they function, or they have functioned in the West, as the domain of cultural re-generation, akin to the domain of education.

§ 196
Nevertheless, the relationship between spectacle and re-creation of culture and the values of that culture is indirect and not a matter that can be easily deciphered. It would be far-fetched to say that spectacles play a crucial role in culture-making; even if

---

12 The film *Portrait of a Stolen Painting* by Raul Ruiz, inspired by Klossowski and loosely based on his *Baphomet*, works out this question of immanence; all paintings point to one other via the technique of *tableaux vivants*, as they open up to a dramatic re-presentation, and all revolve around the absent painting whose theft remains a mystery and to be solved. Matthew Mohr, an installation artist of our times, created an installation piece inspired by this film.

one were to mean grand artistic spectacle or any other grand spectacle, there are many other forces of culture that play their role in re-creation of values. Sometimes, however, a particular spectacle becomes the symbolic spectacle for an epoch, around which all things revolve (for example, the spectacle of Christ on the Cross for the medievals, as Tertullian discusses in his book).

Part III

Grand Artistic Spectacle and the Total Artwork

§ 197

Greek theater is the first example of a grand artistic spectacle in the history of occidental civilization. It is the presentation of a total artwork (where all art forms come together in an organic fusion under the direction of one artist, in this case, the tragic poet) before a huge audience among whom were to be found the leading members of the city-state. The whole theater community was bound together via the dramatic re-creation of the already-known Homeric myths. We do not know even today how all the constituent elements of a performance came together since there is no recording of complete scores and dance choreographies[13] of Greek plays, not to mention evidence for acting and acting styles. We have, however, evidence that Greek dramas were composed and performed as total artworks. What is of utmost significance from a spectacular standpoint is the question as to what held all the arts together in their diversity and even in their opposition; and here again we see the *sympheric* role of the myths. Myths can be painted, sculpted, sung, danced,

---

13 *Gardzienice*, an experimental Polish theater, has done research on Greek music and dance and integrated its findings into its theatrical productions of Greek tragedies. What struck me in the two re-productions of Greek tragedy that they presented in New York City's La MaMa theater was their attempt to revitalize the visceral and the musical aspects of Greek theater, though on a smaller scale.

and finally dramatized and as such functioned as the containing vessel for all the arts.

§ 198
The disintegration of the mythic total artwork does not start with the modern age, but rather with the rise of Greek rationality, with the dissolution of the mythic fabric of ancient Greek culture and, along with these two phenomena, with the dissolution of the temporal structure that corresponds to a mythic world-order (that is a cyclical notion of time, i.e. Nietzsche's eternal recurrence, that is in tune with the cosmic cycle of the renewal of all that is). This gradual dissolution of myth and the Greek theater as an expression of their total artwork is a co-phenomenon to the decay of theater as a grand spectacle, that is, its popularization, which, according to Nietzsche, starts with Euripides. When moderns looked up to the classical age of the Greeks and Romans, they tapped into this phase of Greek culture when myth and theater had already declined. We can then say that moderns simply replicated an already decayed art form or inherited the disintegration of arts and spectacle.

§ 199
In its external features, grand spectacle had existed in antiquity for almost twelve centuries in different forms and historical eras as in the early spectacles of games and different competitions (at Olympia, Delphi, Nemea, and Istmus), in the different phases of Greek and Roman theaters, and the Roman Coliseum, known as the Amphitheatrum Flavium to the Romans. The Coliseum was initiated by Vespasian and completed by Titus and Domitian and dedicated by Titus in 80 A.D. Its inauguration

prompted the first short book of Martial, "A Book of Spectacles," where, referring to the Coliseum, he writes: "All labor yields to Caesar's Amphitheatre: in place of many works, Fame shall speak of one."[33]

§ 200

Spectacular shift from the late Roman to the early Christian era:

Martial: physical movement towards one Grand Spectacle, the Coliseum.

Tertullian: movement away from the physical Grand Spectacle, but spiritual movement towards one purely symbolic Grand Spectacle (Christ on the Cross).

What unifies both world-views is their hegemonic belief in one ultimate Grand Spectacle.

§ 201

If we examine the artistic eras and movements of the past, we see a tendency, a drive towards spectacle-making on a grand scale. This is obviously the case with the tragic Greeks, but is also true, though not on the same level, for the troubadours of Occitan and the Renaissance. The troubadours regarded their poetic activity mostly as performance and wrote their poems in order to sing them before an audience that was diversely constituted (ambiguity, as in *trobar clus*, was a sign of poetic mastery). Although their scope was limited in relation to the grand spectacle of the ancient Greeks, they succeeded, with their spectacles, in kindling sparks in the younger generations of poets who became the harbingers of the modern age. During the Renaissance, although it is known more with its spectacles of visual/plastic arts, all sorts of artistic spectacles flourished and embraced the new age. Whenever and wherever a culture is revitalized in and through artistic activity, a new need for grand spectacle presses itself onto that culture; it is as though the renewed culture were to desire to see its new shape in the mirror.

§ 202

Richard Wagner is the first composer who brought attention to the notion of the total artwork and attempted to revitalize it with success, according to some, and with failure, according to others (including Nietzsche after his break with Wagner). A history of this notion in the modern age needs to be explored since, in my view, total artwork did not lose its relevance to spectacular experiences; on the contrary, in the age of mass culture, it has even become more relevant, though not in the way Wagner formulated it. There are two streaks that culminated in Wagner's version of the total artwork: one streak has to do with Lessing/Winckelmann debate and how Lessing, in his response to Winckelmann's glorification of Greek visual/plastic arts, posits the limitation of each art form vis-à-vis one another despite their independence and freedom in their respective domains.

§ 203

The other streak runs through the Romantics; a call for a total artwork can be read in Tieck, Wackenroder, Novalis, and Brentano, and Schelling who wrote about it, but could not have realized it. Here one can detect the Romantic criticism of classical culture, its logocentricity, and its attempt to put everything under a logical schema including the arts; moreover, the fragmentation of modern culture is also lamented, which also has to do with the Romantic yearning for a spiritual home. In Novalis, for instance, the divergent arts are brought within a unity, "a successful mixture of all the beautiful and living for manifold, total effects."[34] He sees plastic/visual arts, music, and poetry as inseparable elements that can be unified within the same essence of art, but with different relations to each other; he even goes so far to assert that they are synonyms. And he sees poetry as the middle art for all arts, ascribing the function of unification to it and seeing it as *Gemüterregungskunst*[35] (the art that sets the disposition or the emotion): "Poetry is *presentation of disposition—of the inner world in its totality.*"[36] In the final analysis Novalis places the weight on poetry in the order of all arts for the sake of a synthetic artwork.

§ 204
Wagner has, at least, three formulations of the total artwork in his aesthetic writings that span over two decades. The first formulation can be found in *The Artwork of the Future* (1850) in which Wagner defines it as the product of a fusion of the separate phases of art and as a synthesis in which the individual phases contribute each in its own way to the total effect. "Thus the united sister arts," he writes in this work, "will appear, now all together, now in pairs, and again singly, according to the need of the dramatic action, which is the sole criterion…"

§ 205
In his following work, *Opera and Drama* (1850), Wagner gives a detailed picture of what he means by 'total artwork' as he indulges in a verbose micro-analysis. Feuerbach and his sensual materialism are in the background, and, for Wagner, there is a necessity which presents itself of integrating the poetic dialogue,

conceptual speech, into the structure of a dramatic work whose sole appeal is to the emotions. Hence the importance of word-tone synthesis, their organic unity, a central theme of the book. In the Schopenhauerean phase (from 1854 on), Wagner tries to apply Schopenhauer's metaphysics of music to his art (*Tristan and Isolde* is the first Schopenhauerean opera) and at the same time struggles to reconcile his own conception of total artwork with the newly appropriated priority of music. Wagner was convinced all along that the arts alone simply copy the fragmented modern world and, therefore, must come together to create a unified effect. But the dilemma that he was faced with was to understand, show and create in what ways the individual arts are independent and dependent in relation to one another. In the Schopenhauerean phase, the balance tipped towards music, and this posed a theoretical difficulty in Wagner's aesthetics.

§ 206

The second formulation of the total art work is in *Music of the Future*. There Wagner gives more independence to music. According to this account, poetry and music are separate and legitimate forms of art in their own right. Music creates the emotional effect, but presents no answers as to why; it is dramatic poetry that can "give the answers" with the visible performance of a life-like action. Here he still claims that the techniques of writing the verse with music that he presented in *Opera and Drama* are still valid.

§ 207

In the third and final formulation in *Beethoven* (1870) and *The Destiny of Opera* (1871), all other arts are subordinated to music.

Music includes the drama within itself, but not the other way around. Drama can reach its loftiest height and its ideal form only when the poetical visualization of a dramatic action is synthesized with simultaneous musical realization. Hence Wagner defines the ideal drama as a "mimetic-musical improvisation of consummate poetic value" in *The Destiny of Opera*. Furthermore, he argues the possibility of releasing musical composition completely from arbitrary formal patterns by combining it with stage action, or more specifically, with its fixed mimetic improvisation, thus permitting it a freedom of expression subject only to the unique formal requirements which grow from within music itself.

§ 208
After Wagner, many writers, poets, musicians, and artists who heeded the call of their *zeitgeist* paid homage to him and attempted to implement synthesis of all arts in their own domain as they directed their art towards other arts (Baudelaire, Mallarmé, R. Strauss, Artaud and many others).[37]

§ 209
Many art movements of the second half of the nineteenth century and the first quarter of the twentieth century, such as Symbolism, Impressionism, Dadaism, and surrealism, are attempts to re-create total artworks, holistic spectacles and spectators, and integral culture. Poetry and other literature, on the other hand, form the knitting ground for such attempts.

§ 210
But major political movements of the twentieth century either responded negatively to this search for integral art and cul-

ture (as is evident in the Nazi exhibition of "Degenerate Art" or book burnings) or tried to absorb some of its elements for their political agenda and hegemonization of power structures without understanding its authentic, artistic spirit.

§ 211

That the nineteenth-century attempt at synthesis of arts failed to a large extent constitutes no argument against its necessity for culture and its vitality. Wagner failed, because the musician in him took the upper hand; Mallarmé failed because he was only a poet who believed he could idealize a grand spectacle only in his head. These failures are only symptoms of the age and expose the egoistic or the solipsistic modern artist. Total artwork, however, is not an impossibility (ancient Greek poets did create it), but can be created in a different spirit in which a variety of artists from all artistic domains collaborate in an agonistically collective spirit.

§ 212

Whether one artist creates or many artists create a total artwork is irrelevant from a spectacular standpoint. What is of importance is that total artworks exist and have their place in a given culture and its spectacular experiences. On the other hand, one may not be the artist of all arts in a given total artwork, but a coordinator of all arts. For instance, film directors serve this function. The question here is: when it is no longer one artist who creates the entire total artwork, does the *organic* unity of all arts diminish? What, after all, is the organic unity that many artists talk about?

§ 213

Film approximates total artwork but cannot be it since live human presence is missing in film. In our age, in addition to film, certain theater works, performance arts, and installation arts that use performance come close to the total artwork.

§ 214

Let us repeat: a grand artistic spectacle is bringing a great work of art that is a synthesis of all arts (from visual/plastic arts to musical arts), created by one or many artists and spectacle makers, before a grand public, that is, an audience whose members are cultivated to live up to the experience of the spectacle. All of these, of course, are happening in a particular historical period. Furthermore, for a grand artistic spectacle of a total artwork to happen, a variety of spectacular forces must coincide. Such a coincidence, a great happening, is rare indeed, and when it happens, its affects are felt and absorbed by those artistic spirits who are sensitive to the needs of their times.

§ 215

Cultivation of spectators cannot come only from artistic spectacles. Needless to say, each art form can help cultivate the spectators, but the overall artistic education of spectators cannot come from spectacles. Institutions of education and learning, spectators' self-learning and self-cultivation in arts and all the other things that pertain to arts play a crucial role in the formation of a cultivated spectatorship.

§ 216
A grand artistic spectacle must be rich along the horizontal and the vertical axes: it must present or invoke a rich imagery and symbolism (a rich *alphabet* must underlie it) and it must have depth (myths, the flow of the unconscious, help with the deepening of the depth).

§ 217
Under optimum circumstances, a grand artistic spectacle can re-inscribe and restore primary human functions back into culture; such functions as ecstasy (ecstatic connection with oneself and with others), fantasy (the plain in which myths live), emotional integrity (being in touch with one's emotional state), power (knowing one's place in the hierarchy of powers, powers of life), and so on. For such an event to occur, two conditions must be met: at the microscopic level, both the spectacle makers and the spectators have to live up to the moment, and, at the macroscopic level the culture must be ready to take in the affect.

§ 218
A great artwork belongs and, at the same time, does not belong to its creator. It belongs because it carries the sweat, the creative deed, the blood of its creator. And yet, once the work comes into the artistic spectacle, it *belongs* to that audience and to that culture. In the first case, we may wonder as to the *Weltanschauung* of the creator; in the second case, we inquire into what in it has *affect* on the spectators and on culture in general. One can never fully know either, but they remain important questions for a genealogy of spectacle.

§ 219
On the other hand, the merchants, the bourgeois, and the institutions of art claim ownership on works of art for their exchange value and thereby complicate spectacular relations.

§ 220
A certain type of confinement of spectacles takes place at the level of institutionalization of art and artistic spectacles; what this confinement does is to choke off the flow of artistic energies and spirits in and out of spectacles due to arbitrary rules and regulations that come with institutional practices. The following problems can also be added (applicable to art education as well): problems of stagnation, confusion of high and low, absence of the study of classics and the great art works of the past, and absence of creative/original sparks. One more note on the institutionalization of artistic spectacles: for an event that is spiritual (*geistlich*), that is, the spectacle of a work of art, one does not choose spectators according to their finances, but rather according to the artistic demands of that spectacle.

§ 221
Mass media and mass culture have come under criticism by many authors in the post-war (post-1945) era: Adorno and Horkheimer emphasize the instrumental rationality that is the *modus operandi* of the mass media; that is, spectators are instrumentalized by a dominant bourgeois ideology through the mass media. Debord goes one step further when he claims that all spectacular relations are grounded in the metaphysics of the spectacle that operates with an ontological dualism of an active Spectacle, on one side, and a passive spectatorship on the other.

§ 222
Mass media, in its dominant forms and functions, empties out whatever spirit is left from its spectators. And as such, it is the most devastating threat to culture and culture-making.

§ 223
However, the problem does not start or end with the mass media in any of its forms; mass media, on the contrary, is simply an amplification of the mass attitude (or herd mentality) in different types of media. Masses have always existed in every society and all throughout history, and so have their "media" to manifest their attitude. In our age, however, the masses have a louder mouthpiece from which they can spill their attitude to society more effectively.

§ 224
When I say 'masses,' I do not suggest that there are humans who *essentially* belong to the masses. There are traits and tendencies that exist in all in different degrees of strength and that make some more susceptible to the herd mentality; in other words, there are human beings who, due to their background and the absence of cultivation, are more prone to mass appeal than others. I do not dismiss the fact that these traits can be strong, depending on the culture and the personality; I do suggest, however, that these traits must be resisted individually and culturally, if we desire to live in *optimally healthy* societies.

§ 225
What is mass attitude? A mass is not any or every group of spectators who somehow act together in unison. It is, however, typified by certain tendencies some of which are as follows:

- Absence of cultivation of various primary human functions such as thinking and creativity (hence a complacency in the domain of human spirit);
- Firm belief in everyday forms of reality (title, property, political ideology, etc.);
- Gullibility to be an automaton;
- Immediate gratification in most areas of life;
- Appeal to direct and immediate practical functions;
- Bond-making through what is given by society (as convention) and absence of individual re-creation;
- Politics of identity, that is, following an identity that already has a social currency.

§ 226

Therefore, the problem is not that the masses and mass media exist but rather that grand artistic spectacles do not *sufficiently* exist and do not hold their place in the hierarchy of spectacles. All spectacles must be hierarchically organized and point to and look up to grand artistic spectacles in their own cultural and historical contexts. It is a question of power relations among all spectacles.

§ 227

Below is the hierarchy of all spectacles in a specific cultural context that I propose; therefore, when I use the term 'spectacle,' I primarily mean grand artistic spectacle:

Grand artistic spectacles of:

Individual arts   Total artworks   Individual arts

Other artistic spectacles

Other spectacles and mass media

A detailed hierarchy has to be worked out by spectacle makers in their own concrete settings.

§ 228

On the other hand, we should not be tempted to think that artistic spirits, even when they attempt to create a grand artistic spectacle, are free of blemish. Since they too are embedded in their own epoch and do not always overcome its problems, their shortcomings are often reflected in the spectacles they help create. Some problems on the part of spectacle-makers are: the lack of understanding or appropriation of the inner forces of spectacle, treatment of spectators as unintelligent or inartistic, confusion as to the hierarchy of spectacles, confusion as to the hierarchy of outer forces of spectacle within a particular spectacle…

Epilogue

§ 229

There are, no doubt, many chronic problems in today's pathos of spectacle that are exacerbated and perpetuated by the current technological *Dasein* (as Heidegger would say it), the mass media and its instrumental rationality (as Adorno and Horkheimer claim), and the society of the spectacle that operates in the metaphysical split between the active and the passive (according to Debord), or in the S/s cut as I presented. Whatever the problems may be, the starting point and the ending point cannot be where the problems are densely concentrated, as in mass media (or any media that appeal to the masses and are, in turn, abused by them). Debord's limitation is exactly here. In agreement with him, I would state that contemporary pathos of spectacle is shaped, to a large extent, by mass media; but I disagree with his claim that there is nothing but mass media. There have always been masses and creators and also their eternal fight and disagreement. The question is the question of power that Debord avoids asking, and the challenge for the creative, free spirits is to take back what *rightfully* belongs to them.

§ 230

A spectacle can lose its autochthonous spectacular functions and the vitality of its inner and outer forces under, at least, the following circumstances: 1) when it is popularized, that is, when everyday speech gradually takes over the poetic speech of the spectacle (see Nietzsche's criticism of Euripidean drama in *The Birth of Tragedy*); 2) when it is intellectualized the result of which is the stripping down of the non-rational (or less rational) elements of the spectacle; one example in this area is when the theatrical spectacle is reduced to the staging of plot-driven plays as one finds this in Euripides, Roman theater, and early modern theater; 3) when it is subjected to the laws of morality as it becomes a tool for teaching morals to the audience; this is prominent in the morality plays of the fifteenth century as Erich Auerbach lists: "The moralities were plays in which the characters are moral qualities and abstractions of all kinds: Reason, Chastity, Patience, Folly; but also Dinner, Supper, and Paralysis. There are even characters called "Despair of Pardon" and "Ashamed to Confess His Sins"..."[38] 4) when it is subjected to political (or any) ideology either openly or secretly (what the mass media does both in the totalitarian regimes and the liberal democracies of our age).

§ 231

If we survey some of the major artistic movements and their manifestoes of the past century, we will see that they have tried to transform some aspect of spectacular experiences. What did they have to do with the mass media and the masses? The Surrealists, for instance, focused on the unconscious forces and drives and exposed the thin line between fantasy and reality. Artaud was concerned with the emotional intensity and depth of the experience of spectacle, magic, the visceral aspect of spectacle, and the variety of signs (what he called the alphabet of theater) through which it can be manifest. I do not claim here that every artist examines and questions spectacular relations, but every artistic movement does.

§ 232
The biggest challenge in today's age is to get rid of the metaphysical separation, the S/s cut, between the spectacle and spectator and thereby to liberate all the inner and outer forces of spectacle. Most types of mass media re-inscribe this cut perpetually into culture and are the biggest obstacles in the attempts to overcome it.

§ 233
There may be objections to the way I use the term 'art' or 'artistic spectacle.' One objection I hear coming is as follows: I use the term 'art' in a classical way, even following the classical categories of art, but talk about the new, 'post-classical' pathos of spectacle. Isn't there an inconsistency here? You have to develop a theory of art before you can use terms like 'artistic' or 'artist' and presuppose a conception of art. My response: I have not developed a new theory of art, but rely on post-classical theories on art. For one thing, I do not follow the classical notion of the artist who has a certain essence and who is metaphysically separated from others nor the classical definition of art as representation of what is real in any sense of the word and work of art as a product of such representation. Finally, I do agree with Nietzsche's new conception of art that is broad and that pertains to any act of creativity (including re-creation of culture, works of art, one's self and one's relation to others and to the world). Art in the narrow sense as creation of what is considered works of art must be placed on this broader notion of art as creativity. Nietzsche promotes and demotes art at the same time within a post-Kantian framework.

§ 234
In the mid-seventies, Foucault presented his theory of the panopticon[39] where he claims that Occidental civilization shifted, around the turn to the nineteenth century, from the spectacle of punishment to the panopticon in the realm of institutions of punishment and discipline. In this work he explains in-depth the power-truth-knowledge relations in both schemes of institutional formations/practices. In the spectacle of punishment, spectators watch the so-called criminal being tortured in the presence of the powers that be (the King, the Royalty in general, etc.); and through this spectacle the King reinscribes his power back into society (until the whole system starts cracking open). Whereas in the panopticon the gaze bounces back and forth between the Spectacle and the spectator; therefore, the panopticon plays with the boundary of the S/s cut.

§ 235
Although the types of spectacle Foucault talks about in *Discipline & Punish* are not artistic spectacles in the strict sense, they affect our spectacular relations. If one agrees with Foucault of the 1970s that the panopticon shapes our social reality, then one can draw a conclusion from here that the panopticon also shapes our spectacular experiences.

§ 236
Foucault, however, does not apply his power-truth-knowledge analysis to artistic spectacles (since this did not exactly fall within his areas of research interest); this may be intimated in his books on arts. To be able to do such an application, a few points must be kept in mind: for a particular event of artistic spectacle

there exists a body of knowledge, that is, a discourse on that artistic medium, on the artists, and even on that particular spectacle, created by the experts of the field (art critics, historians, etc.); there also exist certain ideas about what art is, what that art form entails (questions of representation, for instance); and finally, that artistic spectacle has affects on its spectators in certain ways (the question of what affects whom). The first is the domain of knowledge and pertains mostly to the experts, the academics, the second, the domain of truth and belongs to the philosophers and theoreticians, and the third, the domain of power belongs to the artists and spectacle makers. Here the type of power that manifests itself is artistic power.

§ 237
Are we in the society of the spectacle?

§ 238
Many different types of spectacles compete over the same territory of spectatorship in a given socio-cultural context. Mass media, artistic spectacles (housed by cinemas, museums, theaters, galleries, concert halls, etc.), scientific spectacles, political spectacles, religious spectacles, and spectacles of sports are some of the most experienced types of spectacles that exist in contemporary society (and here I am following the already accepted categories without dismissing hybrid forms of spectacles). The affects these spectacles have on spectators can be direct or indirect, conscious or unconscious, and quantitative or qualitative. In this sense, one can speak of a *register of spectacle* in the soul, which records all the spectacles that one has experienced.

§ 239

What kinds of affects each type of spectacle has, notwithstanding the particular body of spectators, is a major study area, especially for anthropologists of spectacle. Here some of the questions to explore are: why and how do the mass media produce passivity? Why do spectacles of sports, soccer in particular, produce violence among the fans? Why do political spectacles almost always treat the spectators as an unintelligent, ignorant body of people to be lied to and manipulated? Why do sermons and other religious spectacles, especially in monotheistic religions, treat spectators as blind followers to be agitated into death for a cause or a religious principle or a holy land? These and other related questions, no doubt, have many answers, but they all point to a pathos of spectacle that is full of problems.

§ 240

In all the dominant spectacles of contemporary society listed above, with the exception of artistic and scientific spectacles, spectators are often treated like a herd.

§ 241

In religious spectacles (as in sermons in a variety of religions), the flock needs moral guidance for their lives or religious agitation against a presumed enemy. Youthful minds are already corrupted before they can become individuals.

§ 242

In political spectacles, spectators are treated as mere numbers either for the voting machine (as in political campaigns) or as indicators of the ideal represented by a march or a demonstration. Even if the political ideal may be lofty, the mass treatment of the participants already betrays that ideal. Political expressions in today's society are stagnant, obsolete, demeaning to the individual, and lacking in innovation.

§ 243
Spectacles of sports excite and entertain the masses. There is such a disproportion between, on the one hand, the spirit of playfulness, game, and competition that athletes and all sports people are supposed to embody (but do not, in our age) and, on the other hand, the spiritlessness of their spectators. This, of course, varies from one type of sports to the next, but it seems like the larger the audience, the more it is herd like. Since the passive spectators (passive in relation to game-making) are deprived of sports and competition, they become frustrated and attack one another almost entirely out of context. Soccer fans are the best example of this.

§ 244
Museums take up a significant space in the experience of spectacles of visual and plastic arts for the contemporary spectator. Although seeing an original work of art is an irreplaceable experience, the following problems are endemic to the museum experience: the removal of the work of art from its native fabric (no information can sufficiently create the context, but more can be done in this area), commercialization and bureaucratization of the work of art (there are no foreseeable solutions to this larger problem), uncultivated spectators who have not been initiated into the experience of works of art and who, therefore, do not

make any distinctions among the various ways of *seeing* (spectators can never be cultivated too much).

§ 245
In this book I have established human-made spectacles as my framework and chose not to discuss the difficult topic of spectacles of life, nature, and the cosmos and how they relate to the former. I do not deny the significance of such spectacles in human life; people gather together to watch animals, waterfalls, the eclipse of the sun or the moon, which are all some sorts of spectacles. However, this area fell outside the scope of this work, which focuses on artistic spectacles.

§ 246
In our age, spectacular experiences have become *banal*, and, as a result, many have become desensitized to what they are supposed to experience. There are millions of spectacles made and many of these forced upon spectatorship through the mass media; a one-way communication forces itself onto a complacent, exhausted audience. However, out of all the spectacles made only a few merit thoughtful and imaginative attention. Such proliferation and also banalization of spectacle had perhaps never existed prior to the age of technological reproduction.

§ 247
For the hegemony of the mass media to end, the public domain has to be infused with greatness. This infusion can come about through grand artistic spectacles and their festivals.

§ 248

Since I use the term "the new pathos of spectacle," I owe an explanation to my readers as to what this pathos entails. Before I do so, I would like to talk about what is 'new.' I am in agreement with Nietzsche and some of the post-Nietzscheans in their claim that Occidental civilization had gone through a shift around the beginning of the nineteenth century; the shift has many layers and labels, but is often called the Kantian turning-point or symbolized by the death of God as in Nietzsche. The shift simply signifies that the grounding principles or the highest values of the modern age have been displaced, yielding to the gradually emerging highest values, and this has had impact on all institutions and practices (see Foucault). It is not the place here to delve upon the shift in general. Below is how I understand its impact on its pathos of spectacle in several points:

- There is no one true spectacle that can and will function as the model for all other spectacles (the end of God and platonic idealism).
- Spectacles have their own worth for individuals and cultures and must be cultivated, hence the need for the proliferation of spectacle (the end of the medieval ban on spectacles);
- Spectacles, together and separately, can create a balance between the symbolic and the imagistic registers of the human psyche (the Apollinian-Dionysian oppositional unity);
- Integral spectacles can promote integral human beings and contribute, at a deeper level, to the transformation of

the modern, disconnected lost soul (the legacy of the Romantics and Wagner);
- Spectacles cannot be reduced to functions of rationality, morality, or education or regarded as useful (they may have indirect and deeper connection to the ethos and cultivation of spectators); they have to be rescued from the hegemony of the intellect (Schopenhauer/Nietzsche impact);
- Spectacular experiences have gone through a radical shift in the age of technological reproduction, which opened up the Pandora's box for the masses. The damage of massification can be repaired if the artistic spirits catch up with the damage by re-creating new auras, cults, cultures, and spectatorship, especially in the new artistic media (Benjamin's warning).

§ 249

If there is a new pathos of spectacle that belongs to the post-God epoch, then how did this new pathos emerge? What are some of the discontinuities or ruptures in the previous pathos of spectacle? All throughout this work, I dealt with this problem, namely the new pathos of spectacle and the shift. I can, however, summarize what I consider discontinuities in this area (historically they span over roughly half a century, from 1770 to 1830):

- The idea of total artwork (intimated by Lessing, formulated by the Romantics, tried by Beethoven, and later implemented by Wagner and the Symbolists);
- The beginning of the museum/gallery culture as we know it today;

- Re-invention of *ars erotica* (Sade) and its gradual influence on arts and culture;
- The autonomy of imagination and arts as formulated by Kant;
- The Romantic rebellion against classical culture and its promotion of feelings, emotions, spontaneous expressions as opposed to the supremacy of (classically conceived) reason;
- The primacy of the unconscious (propounded consistently by Schopenhauer);
- The invention of the photographic camera that leads to the experiments with moving images and the invention of the cinematographic camera in late nineteenth century;
- The announcement of the end of history and the end of art (Hegel);
- Goethe's *Faust*.

If we extend the time period further, we can also include:

- The rise of impressionism (Manet, Cezanne, etc.);
- The recovery of the Dionysian (Nietzsche).

§ 250

Many paradigm shifts occur in different art forms; each shift, however, does not necessarily correspond to the epochal shift that is in question or is not the first direct impact of the epochal shift on that art form. And the way these shifts in art forms are named can be misleading from the standpoint of the epochal shift.

Appendix 1

Important Characteristics of the Greek Theater at its Height

This appendix is added to show the prototypical example for artistic spectacles (some of the following points are contested by scholars). Regardless of the type of the artistic spectacle, we can learn from any of these characteristics; if not directly, then indirectly and symbolically:

- The poet was the director of the play and, in early Greek drama, also the actor.
- The poet, among all the makers of the spectacle, was the highest artistic figure without a megalomania (the egoism of the actor, the self-centeredness of the actor, was unknown in early Greek theater).
- The poet did not boast of his artistic achievements (Aeschylus does not even mention the fact that he was a great playwright on his epitaph).
- Poets had to compete with other poets, and the best dramas were chosen in agon or contest (poets were *agonal*). They had to fight with their equals just like in Olympic games before judges and spectators.
- Tragedies were written in tetralogies: three inter-related plays and one satyr play.
- Plots for the tragedies were drawn from Homeric myths, sagas, and epic cycles all of which had place in the mythology of ancient Greeks. The dramatic poets could

modify these myths without deviating too much from the main story.
- Chorus was an essential part of the early Greek drama. According to Nietzsche who emphasizes the origin of theater in the cult of Dionysus, there was nothing but chorus in the earliest tragedies (one can speculate that chorus members dramatized the life of Dionysus based on the stories already known). Unlike various theories of chorus that emphasize the verbal aspect of the chorus, Nietzsche claims that tragic chorus with its singing and dancing is the Dionysian core of the Greek theater. In the next phase, characters, dialogues, and actors were added. Gradually the role of the chorus diminishes, and the Dionysian elements recede into the background.
- Licentiousness and sexual playfulness could be presented on stage within a sacred context, as in satyr plays.
- Masks were used to invoke a variety of figures and deities and to create a sense of ecstatic elevation.
- In early Greek theater, the stage and stage design were minimal and simple.
- Greek theater was an integral form of art and used all art forms available at the time: poetry, music, song, dance, and visual/plastic arts (what Wagner calls *Gesamtkunstwerk*, total artwork). They were organically presented together; in other words, they were coherently unified by way of mythic functions.
- Greek theaters could seat thousands of spectators.
- Plays were performed during festivals that took place once a year.

- Greek theaters were usually built on slopes of hills, as though they were hugging nature.
- Most tragedies included scenes of violence such as murder, the death of the hero, and these scenes were shown and understood within their own contexts (to incite the spectators to violent behavior would be the last thing that would be in the mind of the poet).

Appendix 2

THE UNITY OF SPECTACULAR EXPERIENCES: PROPOSAL FOR A PROGRAM OF ACTION— A MANIFESTO

This project is intended to begin a dialogue between concerned thinkers and artists. It is conceived in the light of contemporary problems in our spectacular experiences in order to take steps towards transformation and rejuvenation of culture. By *spectacular experience*, we mean the relationship between the spectator and the spectacle. The project starts from a simple intuition as to what kind of relationship this is or how it is constituted. We would like to pose this as a question to ponder over the prevailing ways of relating to the spectacle, in the broadest sense of this word, with the chronic problems of our times in mind; some of these problems are enumerated below.

A. Conception of the project: The underlying thoughts that go in the original make-up of this project are as follows: to rejuvenate spectacular experiences towards transformation of culture. To create a spectacle of spectacles so as to be able to live the originary significance of spectacular experience through the unity of spectacles. To rethink and to recreate the configuration of imagery and symbolic experiences.

B. The unity of the spectacle, the spectator and the creator of the spectacle (the poet/playwright, the audience and the stage in ancient Greek drama, see the Omega). The relationship between the spectacle and the spectator as that of:

- feeling,
- sensing,
- seeing/looking,
- hearing,
- relating-to: what kind of relationship is established between the various forces that make up the unity of the spectacle, what kinds of constellations are there between the creators of the spectacle, the spectacle and the spectator? What are some of the contemporary problems in these constellations?
- in body: feelings, instincts and the life of the body; for instance, what kinds of feelings are invoked through the spectacle? How are the creative and destructive instincts played out in the space between the spectacle and the spectator?
- in soul: its image-symbol configuration, what are the issues regarding imagery and symbolic experiences of our times, what is at stake here? Why, in modern times, is an image of violence tied to a symbol of injustice, unlike, for instance, in the ancient tragic spectacle, where an image of violence goes with cosmological principles of justice?
- through language: the way we experience language in concepts and metaphors, the context of poetic language and everyday language, what is the relationship between the spectacle and linguistic experience even if the type of spectacle is non-linguistic such as music?

- reflecting and thinking: how can thinking enter into a meaningful relationship, via the common base of culture, with the process of creativity without interfering in or tampering with that process (i.e. without rationalizing artistic activity),
- knowing: knowledge of the spectacle, its make-up, historical knowledge of spectacular experiences, etc.; how could knowledge of ancient types of spectacles and spectacular experiences, whether those of the Occidental or other civilizations, benefit culture today and contribute to its transformation?
- creating and recreating: how can creativity become a value in culture? Our relationship to the world is, among others, a created relationship; this bond between man and world lives in human creations whether it is works of art or works of culture in general. Since culture itself is created, there is a dynamic relationship between art and culture, as the former provides the models of creativity for the latter. In what ways, then, can the experience of spectacles cultivate creativity? What are some challenges facing the artist today?
- ecstasizing:
- fantasizing through illusions:
- and with spirituality (or in relation to cosmological principles). These pertain to the spectacular experience in the broadest sense.

C. Types of spectacle (in the strict sense of spectacular experience): works of art on display or available for the spectacle (museums, ruins, cities, etc.); theater, dance, music and performance art in general; photography, film, video, TV and other technologies. Classical works as exemplary models vs. products of popular culture as their appropriation (how to bring the two together). Works of art of other cultures and civilizations in these types of spectacles. Different forms of "spectacular" experiences in other civilizations.

Plastic arts ...IA... Film... Theater... PA... Dance... Musical arts
{Image   {Image-Symbol}   {Symbol-Symbol}   Image}

D. Problematic areas in the modern experience of the spectacle in our times:

- The complacent and passive spectator who follows blindly (lack of creativity, appropriation and interactivity),
- Poverty of imagination, magic, mystery and illusion,
- Deficiency in ecstatic disposition (problems in the ecstatic bond between the spectacle and the spectator),
- The missing link to a cosmology,
- Rationalization of the process of creativity,
- Institutionalization of the spectacle (e.g. concert-goers who feel cultured just because they attend concerts),
- Commercialization of the spectacle (due to culture of money or money as the highest value) and the problems with the entertainment industry,
- Narcissism of the stage and the egoism of the modern artist,
- Hegemony of one form of the spectacle over the others whereas they are all necessary,

- Uncultivated (unformed) relation between the spectacle and the spectator (e.g. no selectivity, violence or other things shown to the wrong audience, spectator who does not have a sense of justice).

E. Proposal for an international multi-spectacle festival (see the organizational chart):

An annual festival is here proposed, which will bring artists and artistic groups of all the types of spectacles listed above from all over the world in accordance with the initial platform and based on a theme chosen for that year. This project is a dynamic process, and the festival is not to be considered an end-result of the project, but rather a part of the process.

The thought of bringing together different types of spectacles stemmed from a simple interpretation (or intuition) of the experience of the spectacle; namely, that it presupposes, or exists in, a relationship between the spectacle and the spectator, as the creator of the spectacle entering into a dynamic triangular constellation with the two. Needless to say, but better said, just as there are different types of spectacles and spectators, there are different ways of relations between the two, or different constellations. In the problems listed above, we have also pointed to problems in ways of relating to the spectacle.

By bringing different types of spectacles together, an attempt is being made to achieve the following:

To create a dynamic relationship between the spectacle and the spectator through which creativity is cultivated, as a work of art expects from its spectators. Blind following, crude prejudices, speech impoverished by clichés, lack of both poetic sensibility and rich imagination are some of the obstructions towards establishing creativity as a value.

To rethink the issue of image and symbol and their dynamics. Different configurations of image and symbol on the spectrum of artistic production from plastic arts to musical arts will help recreate these dynamics in the collective soul of our age.

To cultivate and reinscribe the 'illusory' aspect of spectacular experience through which pleasurable and healthy illusions, individual or collective, that lie in the dream-well of the soul are cultivated to make up for loss, suffering and death. That life is joyful despite all.

To develop formations of ecstasy, in relation to and within limits of cosmological justice, by means of which one can see and feel oneself in and with the other, in body and soul. In the domain of "spectacular" experience, this presupposes the "ecstatic" melting-down of the distinction between the spectacle and the spectator. This is the moment where the artist sees himself as the spectator and the spectator as the artist or as part of the spectacle. There are efforts in this direction, especially, in some of the theater movements of our century.

To reshape the spectacle as a depository or outlet of animal instincts (see Artaud). This may be as cruelty, destruction or violence in spectacle to which the spectator is attuned in feelings. To understand and create this in accordance with cosmological principles of creation and destruction, hence with justice.

To make "spectacular" experience a part of the formation of the individual in different stages of life. This can be achieved by developing interactive forms of spectacle, by laying out the process of artistic creativity and tying these to the formative process which entails upbringing and education.

With all of these issues in the agenda, we are proposing an "International Multi-Spectacle Festival" which is composed of various units: the festival itself and its organizing committee, artists who are involved with the artistic aspect of the project, that is, with the production of the spectacle, thinkers who are engaged with the contemplation of the project in its unity, the support group (creation and maintenance of the site, information gathering and dissemination, media, library, etc.), museum (historical and interactive), and school of spectacles.

Endnotes

1. Benjamin talks about cult value of works of art as opposed to their exchange value in his "The Work of Art in the Age of Mechanical Reproduction" in *Illuminations*, tr. by Harry Zohn (New York: Schocken, 1968). The cult value is especially a spectacular function; with the depreciation of work of art, there is also a depreciation of spectacle.

2. *The Birth of Tragedy*, tr. by Walter Kaufmann (New York: Vintage, 1967), section 7.

3. Schiller expresses this idea in his preface to *The Bride of Messina* in which he uses chorus.

4. It was Schiller, as far as I can find out in my research, who introduced the chorus to theater with his *Bride of Messina*.

5. *Theory of Religion* (New York: Zone Books, 1989), 54.

6. According to J. R. Green, "The fifth century Athenian was able to see major theatrical performances twice a year, at a festival called the Lenaia in January and at the City Dionysia in late March. Earlier in the winter period, in December, were celebrations of the Rural Dionysia at local theatres around Attica...We know comparatively little about the Rural Dionysia except that it seems to have originated as an agricultural festival, and historical evidence of a background in a fertility festival is to be seen in the processions with phallus-poles..." *Theatre in Ancient Greek Society* (New York: Routledge, 1994), 6-7.

7. Prometheus, Oedipus, Agamemnon, Medea, Antigone, Orestes and many other tragic characters are all transgressive types; that is, they have transgressed some taboo in relation to one cult, god or goddess, or *nomos* in general, and are consequently pursued by them. In addition, tragic, mythic

figures like satyrs and maenads are transgressive *by nature*, that is, by their intrinsic role in Greek drama.

8   In his essay, "Truth and Lie in an Extramoral Sense," Nietzsche claims that this is how languages are created, insofar as they consist of metaphors and concepts. *Kritische Studienausgabe*, Volume 1 (Berlin: De Gruyter, 1999).

9   *Tableaux Vivants* (Paris: Gallimard, 2007), 131 (translation is mine).

10 Jean-Pol Madou, *Démons et simulacres dans l'oeuvre de Pierre Klossowski* (Paris: Méridiens Klincksieck), 86 (translation is mine).

11 *Such a Deathly Desire*, translated, edited, and with an afterword by Russell Ford (Albany: SUNY Press, 2007), 18.

12 *Ibid.*, 24.

13 *Nietzsche and the Vicious Circle,* p.133.

14 Modern nation-myths do not live up to the universality of ancient myths; in fact, they are disfigured myths (universal mythic symbolism is placed under certain political ideology). This is a central disagreement between Wagner who identifies myths with nationhood and Nietzsche who sees myths as cultural constructs).

15 *On Spectacle*, tr. by T. R. Glover and G. H. Rendall (Cambridge: Loeb Classical Library, 1939), Chapter XXIX, p.295.

16 Ibid., p.297. I cannot give long quotations from Tertullian; I am afraid I would lose my post-classically minded reader. But for those interested in the epochal shift from the pagan to the medieval world and those who can stomach Tertullian's diatribe against pagans, I recommend a closer reading of his book.

17 Section 9.

18 *The Gay Science,* tr. by Walter Kaufmann (New York: Vintage, 1974), Book II, Aphorism 80.

19 *Theater and Its Double,* tr. by M. C. Richards (New York: Grove Press, 1994), "Theater of Cruelty," 85.

20 With pornographic culture, I do not refer to any and every pornography. After all, if we go to the root of the word, porno-graphein is to write about sex, which can be wonderful, elevating, free-spirited. What I have in mind is today's dominant form of pornography that is mostly about money-making, spreading banality, depriving every sacred aspect of sexuality and therefore perpetuating forms of nihilism in the domain of sexuality. I agree neither with the moralists on the questions of presentation of sexuality in spectacle nor with today's pornographists. In addition, here I confine my criticism to pornography in the age of mechanical reproduction.

21 It is not a coincidence that Sade wanted to create erotic spectacles by writing plays, although he is not considered to be a great playwright. He was unable to create by himself a mythic context for his erotic spectacles.

22 LaMothe discusses *theopraxis* in her book *Nietzsche's Dancers* (New York: Palgrave MacMillan, 2006).

23 *World as Will and Representation,* tr. E. F. J. Payne (New York: Dover, 1969), by Volume 1, Chapter 52.

24 *Ibid.,* 264.

25 *The Birth of Tragedy,* 55.

26 *This is not a Pipe,* tr. by J. Harkness (Los Angeles: University of California Press, 1983), 32.

27 *Ibid.,* 34.

28 In this regard, one may refer to Vernant and Vidal-Naquet's *Myth & Tragedy,* tr. by J. Lloyd (New York: Zone Books, 1988)

where they give numerous examples of ambiguity from Sophocles' tragedies.

29 Ibid., 43.

30 *The Gay Science,* Aphorism 341, *Thus Spoke Zarathustra,* and *The Will to Power.*

31 *Confessions,* tr. by G. Wills (New York: Penguin Books, 2006), Book XI.

32 *Cinema,* tr. by H. Tomlinson and B. Habberjam (Minnesota: The University of Minnesota Press, 1986), Vol. 1, 103.

33 Martial, *Epigrams,* tr. by G. Wills (New York: Viking, 2008), "Book of Spectacles."

34 Novalis *Werke,* "Fragmente und Studien 1797-1798," Fragment 26, p. 382, (translation is mine).

35 *Ibid.,* "Fragmente und Studien 1798-1800," Fragment 128, p.544.

36 *Ibid.,* Fragment 141, p.547.

37 They all paid homage to Wagner as a pioneer in this area, but did not refrain from criticizing him and showing his failures and limitations, and came up with their own version of synthesis of all arts: for example, *correspondence* in Baudelaire and *L'Oeuvre* in Mallarmé.

38 *Introduction to Romance Languages and Literature* (New York: Capricorn Books, 1961), 114.

39 *Discipline & Punish,* tr. by A. Sheridan (New York: Vintage, 1995).

www.ingramcontent.com/pod-product-compliance
Lightning Source LLC
Chambersburg PA
CBHW022012160426
43197CB00007B/397